the **complete** *series*

Gluten-free

& multi-allergy cookbook

Lola Workman

R&R PUBLICATIONS MARKETING PTY LTD

Published by
R&R Publications Marketing Pty Ltd
ABN 78 348 105 138
PO Box 254, Carlton North
Victoria 3054, Australia
Phone: (61 3) 9381 2199
Fax: (61 3) 9381 2689
Email: info@randrpublications.com.au
Website: www.randrpublications.com.au
Australia-wide toll-free: 1800 063 296

©Lola Workman

The Complete Gluten-free & multi-allergy cookbook

Author: Lola Workman
Publisher: Anthony Carroll
Designer: Aisling Gallagher
Food Stylist: Elly Cavell, Neil Hargreaves, R&R Photostudio
Food Photography: Paul Nelson, R&R Photostudio
Recipe Development: Lola Workman
Proofreader: Stephen Powell

Cover recipe *Baps* on page 138

ISBN 978-1-74022-742-1

Printed September 2010
Printed in China

Contents

Introduction

The first step with allergy cookery is to recognise and memorise the list of foods that can be included in your diet. Your dietician or doctor will provide a list of the foods you must avoid and this book will help you select ingredients to replace those foods.

Once you have this information you will soon become accustomed to reading the labels of every product, that you buy. Never buy a mixed product such as gluten-free flour, that does not specify the ingredients. In Australia it is law that such products must contain this information. A product may be gluten-free, but can still include milk products or other chemicals or ingredients that you cannot tolerate.

Using these recipes you will be able to produce a nutritional diet that will also satisfy your palate. If you have not tried to make such things as crumpets or pan breads previously, don't worry, just follow the instructions step by step. The method used in these recipes is different from wheat flour cookery, so please follow these methods carefully.

Remember that when you are making bread, homemade bread is not meant to keep fresh more than one day – in years gone by bread was baked every day and

in country areas it still is. The ingredients that are added to commercial breads to extend the shelf life are chemicals and additional gluten, ingredients we want to avoid. You will find that once you get organised, you will enjoy the challenge of producing fresh, chemical-free foods.

Pre-mixes can be weighed in exact quantities, then bagged and kept in your cupboard until you are ready to bake. When you are blending your own flour, always mix at least 3kg (6lb) at a time and store it in a large calico bag so it will keep indefinitely for you. We have stored flour using this method for 4 years and it was still fresh and ready to use.

Nutritional value of ingredients

Amaranth flour – Extremely high in nutritional value, amaranth flour is higher in protein than most commonly used grains, with the exception of quinoa. It has a near perfect balance of amino acids, and is very high in fibre, iron, manganese, phosphorus and magnesium. It also has a high content of calcium, pantothenic acid, potassium, protein, vitamin B6 and zinc. Unlike most grains, amaranth is high in vitamin C and also contains vitamin A.

Fine rice flour – Rice originated in Asia but is now grown in many different parts of the world. It differs from most other

cereals as it needs to be planted on land that is submerged with water, though some varieties do grow in upland areas. Rice is a good source of carbohydrates, but doesn't have quite as much protein as some other cereals. Rice flour, because of the lack of gluten, cannot be used to make a yeasted loaf, but can be used for cakes, biscuits and pancakes. Rice flakes, both brown and white, can be added to muesli or made into a milk pudding or porridge.

Tapioca starch – Milled from the dried starch of the cassava root (a woody perennial shrub native to Brazil and Paraguay, now widely grown in the tropics and subtropics) tapioca starch is recovered by wet-grinding the washed roots and continuous re-washing – resulting in a pure carbohydrate. The starch grains, once released from the strained pulp, are dried to a paste then milled into flour. The unmodified starch is called native tapioca starch or native tapioca flour and is a fine white powder. Best used in combination with other flours, it is gluten-free and easy to digest.

Potato flour and starch – Although tapioca starch is often used to replace arrowroot in recipes, they are slightly different, but as they are both clear starches they are usually interchangeable.

Potatoes are dried and then ground to a powder to make this flour, which is high in carbohydrates. It is also a good source of vitamin B6, iron, zinc, niacin, potassium, manganese, magnesium, phosphorus, thiamine, vitamin C and fibre.

Besan flour – Besan flour is called dhal flour or channa dahl in India, while in England and most of Europe it is known as gram flour. The highest quality flour comes from India and is golden in colour with no brown specs of skin.

Made from roasted chickpeas, which are very high in protein, besan flour is a wonderful source of fibre and contains most vitamins and minerals. It also contains lots of fabulous antioxidants. Chickpeas are high in complex carbohydrates, meaning they provide energy over a long period, making them a great help for diabetics as they produce little demand on insulin.

Blending your own flour

Formulation of these recipes came as a result of my cookery classes for food intolerance for those who cannot tolerate wheat or gluten in their diets. I have avoided using soya bean flour as many people are intolerant to it and children particularly don't like the strong taste.

Nutrition should be considered when you are selecting a gluten-free replacement for wheat flour as simple mixes of rice and cornflour do not provide enough nutrition to replace wheat, particularly for children.

My bread and pastry flour can be used in all recipes to replace all-purpose flour – important if you are intolerant to corn or salicylates. This flour is lighter and drier so if you are using it for cakes, 1 tablespoon of almond meal or other nut meal to each 100g of flour will increase the moisture level.

Although all recipes in this book were thoroughly tested using the superfine flour blend, any of these blends can be used in most of the recipes in this book. Some will give a better result than others, depending on the recipe, but they can all be used for both my sauce blocks and for cookies and pastry. Select the blend that suits your dietary requirements and continue using this blend throughout.

Lola's all-purpose flour

400g (14oz) besan flour
400g (14oz) maize cornflour
200g (7oz) potato flour
200g (7oz) yellow maize flour

Lola's bread and pastry flour

400g (14oz) besan flour
400g (14oz) potato flour
200g (7oz) fine rice flour
200g (7oz) arrowroot

Superfine flour

200g (7oz) besan flour
200g (7oz) potato starch
150g (5oz) tapioca starch
100g (3½ oz) fine rice flour

Grain-free blend

200g (7oz) besan flour
200g (7oz) tapioca starch
100g (3½ oz) potato starch
100g (3½ oz) buckwheat flour or
   amaranth flour

Potato-free blend

200g (7oz) white sorghum flour
200g (7oz) fine white rice flour
100g (3½ oz) brown rice flour
100g (3½ oz) arrowroot

See **easy blending method** on page 8

Easy blending method

Weigh the ingredients. **Step 1**

Place them into a large plastic bag and shake well. **Step 2 and 3**

Place a large sieve in another bag. **Step 4**

Shake the bag from side to side to sift the flour, press out any lumps. **Step 5**

The flour is now ready for use. Store in paper or calico bags. Do not store in airtight containers. **Step 6**

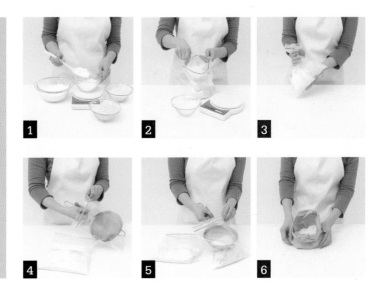

Sauce blocks

I created these blocks years ago for my cookery classes to simplify sauce making. They have proved invaluable as a replacement for milk in producing a basic, dairy-free sauce that has many uses. This sauce can be used as a base for your own preservative-free baby food, to prevent quiche curdling in a hot oven, or to make a creamy dairy-free soup. Once you have tried them you will never be without them in your freezer.

200g (7oz) dairy-free margarine
   or 1 cup olive oil
200g (7oz) flour blend of choice (page 7)

1 Melt the margarine or heat oil in a saucepan over a low heat. Using a wooden spoon, stir in the flour.

2 Continue stirring and cook for about 3 minutes until the mixture slides in the saucepan.

3 Pour the mixture into a 12-hole iceblock tray, then freeze until required.

breakfast & brunch

We take for granted that breakfasts and brunches give us a great start to the day, especially if you do not have a problem with wheat based foods. But spare a thought for those amongst us who suffer a wheat or gluten allergy. This chapter has been written to give all of us a great start to the day, by providing alternatives to store bought breads and breakfast foods.

Amaranth porridge

½ teaspoon salt
1 cup amaranth breakfast cereal
½ cup milk

1 Place 1½ cups of cold water and salt in a saucepan and bring to the boil. While stirring the water add the amaranth cereal in a steady stream.
2 Cook for about 2 minutes, add the milk, stir and cook until smooth.
3 Serve hot with stewed prunes and candied peel.

Amaranth cereal is made from the flowerets of a broad-leafed plant from South America. A centuries-old herb used by Aztecs and American Indians, it is higher in protein than wheat, corn or soya beans. According to the statistics on the packaging it is high in dietary fibre, as well as vitamins, calcium and many minerals. Apart from this it actually tastes good, with a mild nutty flavour so it is an ideal cereal for children, as well as adults.

Serves 1 • Preparation 5 minutes • Cooking 6 minutes

Thai porridge

½ cup large tapioca soaked in 1 cup boiling water overnight
1 cup milk (skim, full cream or rice)
1 tablespoon sugar
1 tablespoon shredded coconut

1 Place the soaked tapioca in a saucepan over high heat. Add milk, stirring constantly until it boils.
2 Reduce the heat and simmer for 20 minutes. Add the sugar and shredded coconut to the porridge. (A whisked egg can be added here for extra nutrition.)
3 Cook gently for one more minute. Serve warm with yoghurt, honey and chopped cashew nuts.

Serves 2 • Preparation 10 minutes • Cooking 30 minutes

Poha porridge

1 teaspoon psyllium
pinch salt
½ cup rolled poha flakes
½ cup milk

1 In a small bowl place ½ cup cold water and the teaspoon of psyllium. Let stand about 2 minutes.
2 Place 1 cup of water and the salt in a saucepan and bring to the boil.
3 While stirring the water add the poha flakes in a steady stream.
4 Cook for about 2 minutes, add the psyllium mixture and milk. Stir and cook until smooth. Serve hot with milk and brown sugar.

Poha is a fine-rolled rice flake thicker than baby rice cereal but thinner than the traditional hard-rolled rice flakes. The poha cooks quickly for an easy morning porridge. It is available from health food stores or Indian food shops.

Serves 1 • Preparation 5 minutes • Cooking 8 minutes

Dairy-free hotcakes

2 eggs
¼ cup lemonade or soda water
2 teaspoons vanilla essence
2 tablespoons olive oil
3½ oz/100g Lola's superfine flour (page 7)
2 tablespoons caster sugar
2 teaspoons gluten-free baking powder
½ cup extra oil to grease crumpet rings

1 Grease a flat pan or skillet with a little olive oil. Separate the eggs, put the two yolks in a medium-sized mixing bowl and retain the whites to beat separately.

2 Add the lemonade, vanilla essence and oil to the egg yolks. Combine the flour, caster sugar and baking powder and whisk in the liquids using a wire whisk. Set aside.

3 Whisk the two egg whites with a rotary or electric beater until stiff. Stir the stiffened egg into the hotcake batter and whisk well. Pour into a jug for easier handling while cooking.

4 Place some oil in a small pie tin to oil the crumpet rings. Heat the pan on medium heat. Pour about half a cupful of batter into crumpet rings in the greased pan. Let cook until the batter is set. Turn once to cook other side.

5 Serve warm with honey or syrup. These hotcakes freeze well in a plastic container or wrapped in foil.

Free of corn, wheat, soy, gluten and dairy, I use crumpet rings to regulate the size of the hotcakes as they are made from a thin batter. If you don't have crumpet rings use a small omelette pan.

Serves 1 • Preparation 10 minutes • Cooking 7 minutes

Bacon and egg waffles

1 cup milk
5½ oz/160g Lola's superfine flour (see page 7)
1 teaspoon gluten-free baking powder
¼ cup olive oil
¼ cup parsley, chopped
salt and freshly ground black pepper
2 rashers bacon or ham, rind removed and finely chopped
2 eggs

1 Brush the waffle iron with oil and heat to manufacturer's instructions. Place the milk into a bowl and sift in the flour and baking powder.

2 Mix with a whisk to ensure a smooth batter. Add the oil, parsley, salt and pepper. Add the bacon or ham to the batter.

3 Beat the eggs until light and fluffy and stir into the mixture. The batter should be very thin so that it will quickly and easily cover the waffle iron.

4 Pour mix into waffle iron and cook according to the manufacturer's instructions. Repeat until mix is all used, stirring prior to each pour to maintain consistency. These waffles freeze well wrapped in foil.

Free of corn, wheat, soy and gluten. You will need an electric waffle iron to cook the waffles.

Serves 2 • Preparation 7 minutes • Cooking 5 minutes

Breakfast on the run

1 cup rolled rice flakes
1 tablespoon psyllium
½ cup dried apricots, chopped
1 tablespoon gluten-free baking powder
5½ oz/160g Lola's superfine flour (page 7)
1 cup puffed amaranth cereal
½ cup desiccated coconut
½ cup cashew nuts, chopped
2 oz/60g ground sunflower kernels
1 cup sultanas
2 tablespoons honey
4 oz/125g brown sugar
¼ cup olive oil
1 egg, beaten

1 Preheat the oven to 320°F/160°C. Line a 7 x 10 x 1 in/18 x 26 x 3cm deep baking tin with baking paper. Place the rice flakes, psyllium, apricots and 2 cups of water in a covered microwave dish and cook for 3 minutes in the microwave oven.

2 Add remaining ingredients to the cooked rice flake and apricot mixture. Stir well to combine ingredients and press into the baking tin and bake for 20 minutes.

3 Remove from oven, cut into bars, separate and place on a baking tray. Return to oven and cook for a further 20 minutes, let cool on the tray, then wrap and refrigerate until required.

Free of corn, wheat, soy, gluten and dairy. This nutritious slice is perfect for a quick breakfast with a cup of coffee. It keeps well in the refrigerator for up to two weeks – a great stand by.

Serves 2 • Preparation 20 minutes • Cooking 45 minutes

Date and ginger breakfast bars

½ cup wholemeal rolled rice flakes
pinch salt
2 tablespoons rice or maple syrup
1 tablespoon sugar-free apricot jam
1 teaspoon almond essence
1 cup dates, chopped
2 oz/60g desiccated coconut
2 oz/60g shredded coconut
2 oz/60g crystalised ginger, chopped
2 oz/60g ground almonds
2 tablespoons rice flour
1 tablespoon psyllium

1 Line a 9 x 3 in/22 x 8cm slice tin with baking paper. Place the rice flakes, salt and 7 oz/200mL of cold water into a deep microwave dish. Cover and microwave on high for 3 minutes, then let stand for 3 minutes.

2 Add the rice flake mixture to other ingredients, mix well and press into the prepared tin. Bake for 20 minutes.

3 Remove from the oven and cut the mixture into four bars. Place the cut bars back into the oven on a baking tray and bake for a further 20 minutes, turning once. Let cool before wrapping.

These great breakfast bars are ideal for snacks and take-out lunches. They will keep for at least two weeks in the refrigerator.

Makes 4 bars • Preparation 10 minutes • Cooking 50 minutes

French toast

1 egg
¼ cup milk
2 slices bread

Savoury toast
salt and freshly ground black pepper

Sweet toast
1 tablespoon sugar
1 teaspoon vanilla essence
½ teaspoon ground cinnamon

1 Whisk together the egg and milk. For savoury toast, add salt and pepper to the mixture and whisk well. For sweet toast, add sugar, vanilla essence and cinnamon to the mixture and whisk well.
2 Melt a nob of butter in a frying pan. Dip the bread slices in the egg mixture, covering both sides. Place in the heated pan and cook for a few minutes, both sides over medium heat.
3 Serve with your favourite breakfast spread.

You will need two slices of my sandwich bread or any gluten-free bread for this recipe.

Serves 1 • Preparation 7 minutes • Cooking 6 minutes

Potato cakes

1 egg
1 potato, unpeeled and coarsely grated
2 tablespoons Lola's superfine flour (page 7)
salt and freshly ground black pepper

1 Lightly whisk the egg and add to the grated potato. Fold in the flour, salt and pepper. Heat a small amount of oil in a shallow pan. Fry over a medium heat until golden, turning once. Serve with baked beans, sautéed mushrooms or tomatoes and sprinkle with salt flakes.

Chopped bacon or ham can be added for extra flavour.

Serves 1 • Preparation 5 minutes • Cooking 5 minutes

Apricot and almond muffins

1 tablespoon gelatine
2 tablespoons psyllium
3½ oz/100g dried apricots, chopped
5 oz/150g Lola's all-purpose flour (page 7)
2 eggs
2 oz/60g brown sugar
½ cup olive oil
1 teaspoon vanilla essence
1 teaspoon almond essence
1 tablespoon gluten-free baking powder
2 oz/60g ground almonds

1 Preheat the oven to 360°F/180°C. Grease a 6-cup muffin pan or line the pans with muffin papers. Sprinkle the gelatine and psyllium on 1 cup of cold water and let stand for a few minutes. Sprinkle the dried apricots with a little flour to separate.

2 Beat the eggs and sugar in a large bowl until thick and creamy. Add the gelatine and psyllium mixture. Stir the oil and essences into the mixture, then the flour and baking powder. Fold in the chopped apricots and ground almonds.

3 Spoon into the pans and bake for 20–25 minutes, depending on the size of the muffin pans.

With the brown sugar and ground almonds these muffins are not light and fluffy but are great for a nutritious breakfast. They freeze well in a plastic container.

Makes 6 • Preparation 12 minutes • Cooking 25 minutes

Fruit muffins

3 tablespoons sugar
1 tablespoon psyllium
1 tablespoon gelatine
1 tablespoon dried yeast
2 egg whites
1 teaspoon salt
½ teaspoon citric acid
8 oz/250g Lola's superfine flour (page 7)
2 tablespoons olive oil
1 cup mixed fruit

1   Grease a muffin tray or line the pans with muffin papers. Place 1 cup of cold water into a large glass bowl or microwave dish. Add the sugar, psyllium and gelatine. Let stand for 1 minute to soften.

2   Heat the gelatine mixture in the microwave for 50 seconds. Add the yeast and stand for 10 minutes. Whisk the egg whites, salt and citric acid in a separate bowl with an electric mixer until stiff. Tip the dry ingredients into the wet mixture.

3   Beat in the oil and whisked eggs for 1 minute with electric mixer. Cover and let stand again for 10 minutes.

4   Preheat the oven to 360°F/180°C. Spoon a tablespoon of the mixture into the tins, sprinkle with half the fruit, add more batter, then sprinkle with remaining fruit, top with mixture and leave until puffy – about 15 minutes. Place in the centre of the oven and bake for 20 minutes. Remove from the oven and wrap in a clean tea towel to cool, remove muffins from the pans, then place in a plastic bag until ready to serve.

Makes 8 • Preparation 35 minutes • Cooking 22 minutes

English muffins

¼ cup olive oil
1 tablespoon glycerine
2 tablespoons gelatine
2 tablespoons dried egg white
1 teaspoon citric acid
2 teaspoons salt
2 teaspoons sugar
2 tablespoons dried yeast
18 oz/500g Lola's superfine flour (page 7)
1 tablespoon mixed spice
1 cup mixed fruit
1 apple, finely chopped

1 Preheat the oven to 400°F/200°C. Grease the Yorkshire pudding trays with margarine. Place 2 cups of warm water, oil and glycerine into large mixing bowl. Add the dry ingredients to the liquids and mix well for about 1 minute.

2 Cover the bowl with a large plastic bag and leave to rise for 10–15 minutes. Beat the mixture for 1 minute. Fold in the fruit and spoon into muffin trays.

3 Leave the mixture to rise for 20 minutes or until it is puffy. Bake on the middle shelf for 25 minutes. Remove from oven and wrap in a clean tea towel to cool, then place in a sealed plastic bag until ready to use.

These muffins are cooked in large muffin tins. A flat top is achieved by placing a scone tray on top of the rising muffins 10 minutes into the baking time.

Makes 6 • Preparation 40 minutes • Cooking 25 minutes

Banana and blueberry muffins

7 oz/200mL milk
1 teaspoon salt
1 tablespoon gelatine
3½ oz/100g caster sugar
1 tablespoon dried yeast
2 eggs
1 ripe banana
2 tablespoons rice syrup or honey
2 tablespoons olive oil
6 oz/160g Lola's superfine flour (page 7)
1 tablespoon psyllium
1 cup fresh blueberries

1 Grease a 12-cup muffin tray or line with muffin papers. Place milk in a large microwave-proof mixing bowl. Add salt, gelatine and 1 tablespoon of the caster sugar. Let stand for a few minutes, and then heat in microwave for 1 minute on high.

2 Stir the yeast into the warm milk mixture and leave to stand for 20 minutes. Lightly beat the eggs. In a small bowl, mash the banana and add the rice syrup, olive oil and eggs. Blend this mixture until smooth.

3 Combine the two wet mixes in the large bowl and add the flour, psyllium, and remaining caster sugar. Mix well, cover the bowl and leave to rise for 20 minutes.

4 Preheat the oven to 360°F/180°C. Fold in the blueberries and spoon the mixture into the muffin tins. Leave to rise for another 20 minutes before baking. Bake muffins for 30 minutes. Remove from oven and wrap in a clean tea towel to cool.

Makes 12 • Preparation 1 hour 15 minutes • Cooking 30 minutes

Pumpkin scones

1 tablespoon psyllium
1 egg
1 tablespoon milk for egg wash
½ cup olive oil
1 tablespoon honey
2 oz/60g cooked mashed pumpkin
10½ oz/300g Lola's all-purpose flour (page 7)
2 tablespoons milk powder
1 teaspoon nutmeg
2 tablespoons gluten-free baking powder
1 teaspoon salt

1 Preheat the oven to 440°F/220°C. Grease a baking tray or cover with baking paper. Add the psyllium to ¼ cup cold water and let stand to form a jelly.

2 To make egg wash without using an additional egg, lightly whisk the egg in a small mixing bowl, then tip the egg into a large mixing bowl to use in the scone mixture. Add 1 teaspoon milk to the small bowl, mix to combine with the egg residue with the pastry brush and you have egg wash to glaze the scones.

3 Add the oil and honey to the mashed pumpkin and stir in the psyllium jelly, egg and 2 tablespoons hot water. Place the flour, milk powder, nutmeg, baking powder and salt into the mixture and fold with a table knife to combine to a soft dough. Do not mix more than necessary.

4 Place a little extra flour on a piece of cling wrap, tip the soft scone dough on to it, cover with wrap and knead gently. Uncover lightly oil your fingers and press out in a thick slab, then cut into six thick scones. Place on the baking tray and glaze with the egg wash. Bake on a high shelf for 15–20 minutes. Remove the scones from the oven and wrap in a damp tea towel to cool.

Serves 2 • Preparation 25 minutes • Cooking 20 minutes

Plain scones

1 tablespoon psyllium
1 egg
2 tablespoons butter
8 oz/250g Lola's bread and pastry flour (page 7)
1 tablespoon gluten-free baking powder
3½ oz/100g arrowroot
2 teaspoons gelatine
2 tablespoons pure icing sugar

1 Preheat the oven to 400°F/200°C. Grease a baking tray or cover with baking papers. Add the psyllium ¼ cup of cold water and let stand to form a jelly.

2 To make an eggwash without using an additional egg, lightly whisk the egg in a small mixing bowl, then tip the egg into the psyllium mixture. Add 2 teaspoons of water to the mixing bowl, mix to combine.

3 Lightly whisk the egg and psyllium mixture, then add ½ cup warm water and butter. Continue mixing, then add the remaining dry ingredients. Combine well with a knife and if still too sticky turn out onto a floured plastic sheet to knead in a little extra flour, or fine rice flour.

4 Cut out using an oiled cutter and place on the prepared tray, glaze with egg wash and bake for 10–15 minutes. Wrap in a tea towel to cool.

Serves 2 • Preparation 20 minutes • Cooking 15 minutes

Fluffy pikelets

2 eggs
2 tablespoons olive oil
1 teaspoon vanilla essence
¼ cup lemonade or warm water
3½ oz/100g Lola's all-purpose flour (page 7)
2 level teaspoons gluten-free baking powder
1 tablespoon psyllium
2 tablespoons milk powder

1 Separate the eggs, place the yolks in a large bowl and whites in a small bowl to be beaten later. Add the olive oil, vanilla essence and lemonade or water to the yolks and whisk lightly. Whisk the dry ingredients into the liquid mixture. Beat the egg whites until firm and whisk into the batter. Leave to stand as you prepare the pan.

2 Burn 1 teaspoon of butter in a small pan. Wipe out with kitchen paper and grease again with a small amount of butter. Adjust the heat under the pan to a low temperature. This important step will ensure even cooking of the pikelets with any pan, even one with a non-stick surface.

3 Regulate the heat to low under the prepared pan. Place a small amount of batter into the pan using a ladle or a small jug to pour the batter. If the mixture is too thick to pour, add a little more warm water. Cook the pikelet until it starts to bubble and looks firm on top. Turn with a spatula and cook for just a few seconds on the other side. Remove from the pan and keep covered with foil or a cloth until ready for use.

Even non-stick pans need to be seasoned to cook pikelets made with gluten-free flour. An electric frypan needs only a light oiling as the heat is regulated.

Serves 2 • Preparation 12 minutes • Cooking 8 minutes

Buckwheat pancakes

2 tablespoons egg replacer
2 teaspoons agar powder
2 tablespoons olive oil
3 oz/90g Lola's all-purpose (page 7)
2 tablespoons buckwheat flour
2 teaspoons gluten-free baking powder
2 tablespoons rice milk

1 Beat the egg replacer, agar and $\frac{1}{3}$ cup warm water with an electric beater until frothy then continue beating until thick and creamy. Using a wire whisk, fold in the oil, flours and baking powder. Add the rice milk and whisk well until the mixture is a smooth batter. It should be thin enough to pour and cover the bottom of the pan – if not add a little more warm water.

2 Grease a flat pan or skillet and place it on a medium heat. Pour in enough mixture to thinly coat the bottom of the pan. Lift the pan and tilt to help spread the mixture evenly over the pan base.

3 Cook until the top is firm. Turn with an egg slice and cook the other side. Cover with a cloth or place in a plastic bag to prevent drying. Serve with stewed apple or rhubarb sprinkled with cinnamon sugar. The pancakes will freeze well wrapped in foil. Thaw before reheating to serve.

Serves 2 • Preparation 8 minutes • Cooking 8 minutes

Crumpets

1 teaspoon sugar
1 teaspoon salt
1 tablespoon dried yeast
1 tablespoon psyllium
1 tablespoon olive oil
8 oz/250g Lola's bread and pastry flour (page 7)
3 teaspoons gluten-free baking powder

1 Place 1 cup of warm water, sugar and salt in a bowl and stir in the yeast. Let stand for about 5 minutes or until bubbles appear and the mixture is frothy. In another bowl, add the psyllium to ¼ cup cold water and let stand until it becomes a jelly. Use a flat-bottomed dish or cake tin with about 1 cup of oil to grease the rings between cooking of the crumpets. Use a small pair of tongs to handle the hot rings.

2 Combine the yeast and psyllium mixtures and add the olive oil and flour. Finally, add the baking powder and beat well with an electric mixer to distribute the yeast – if the mixture is too thick to pour, add a little more warm water.

3 Heat the pan and grease well, then grease the rings and place in the pan. Using a jug, pour in enough mixture to half fill the ring. Cook on medium heat until the mixture starts to bubble and set. Remove the ring and continue to cook on low heat until set; turn the crumpet. Lightly brown until the top is just coloured. You can use a lid to cover the cooking crumpets that will allow them to cook without turning. Repeat until all the batter is used.

4 Cool and pack in cling wrap and refrigerate until ready to use. The crumpets will keep for a week wrapped in the refrigerator. Toast and serve with honey.

Serves 2 • Preparation 15 minutes • Cooking 15 minutes

Basic crêpes

1 egg
1 cup milk
3½ oz/100g Lola's all-purpose flour (page 7)
1 tablespoon olive oil
juice of ½ lemon

1 Beat the egg and half the milk together. Add the sifted flour and the oil and beat until a smooth batter forms. Thin with the remainder of the milk. Let stand for a few minutes and adjust the consistency to a thin batter with additional water if required. Finally, add the lemon juice. Leave to stand while you prepare the crêpe pan.

2 Burn 1 teaspoon of butter in a flat pan. Wipe out with kitchen paper and grease again with a small amount of butter. Adjust the heat under the pan to a low temperature. This important step will ensure even cooking of the crêpes with any pan, even one with a non-stick surface.

3 Pour a very thin layer of batter into the pan and then tilt the pan quickly to give a good coverage. By the time the pan is covered the crêpe should be set, if not the batter is too thick. To correct, add a little more water.

4 With a spatula, carefully ease the crêpe from the edge of the pan and flip it over to cook the other side for a few seconds.

As each crêpe is cooked, slide it onto a plate or piece of foil and cover with a cloth to prevent drying.

Makes 2 cups • Preparation 10 minutes • Cooking 10 minutes

Polenta porridge

½ cup fine polenta
½ cup milk
salt to taste

1 Place 1 cup of boiling water in a saucepan on high heat and boil rapidly. While briskly stirring the water with a wooden spoon, trickle the polenta into the saucepan in a fine steady stream.
2 Continue stirring until it is thick and cooked, about 2 minutes. Stir in the milk and serve hot with yoghurt or creamy milk. Season with salt as desired.

Serves 1 • Preparation 5 minutes • Cooking 8 minutes

Dairy-free frittata

3 or 4 large mushrooms
1 brown-skinned potato, unpeeled and sliced
½ cup peas or beans

Basic sauce
2 sauce blocks (page 9)
salt and freshly ground black pepper
3 beaten eggs or replacer

1 To make the basic sauce, place 1 cup of boiling water in the saucepan, add the sauce blocks and let stand until soft. Return to the heat and whisk until it thickens. Season with salt and pepper. Remove from the heat and add the beaten eggs or replacer. Stand aside. Steam the sliced potatoes until tender and cook the peas or beans in boiling, salted water for 3 minutes.

2 In a frying pan sauté the mushrooms in a small amount of dairy-free margarine. Add the sliced potatoes and peas or beans, and fry for a few minutes to brown the potato.

3 Pour the sauce mixture over the vegetables, reduce the heat and cook for about five minutes. Place the pan under a hot grill for 10 minutes to set the egg mixture. Serve immediately.

You can use left over vegetables for this dish.

Serves 1 • Preparation 8 minutes • Cooking 15 minutes

lunch &
dinner

Celiac disease is reputed to affect one in every 100 Australians, but is greatly under diagnosed. With these figures in mind it is no wonder that many of us are looking to change our eating habit. In this chapter we offer a great range of suitable alternatives – tested and tasty recipes that the whole family will enjoy.

Fish fingers

1 lb/500g boneless fish fillets
½ cup potato starch
2 tablespoons egg replacer
1 cup fine rice crumbs

1 Mince the fish fillets and press the meat into an ice-block tray. Freeze for at least 2 hours, or overnight.
2 Place the potato starch in a plastic bag and beat the egg replacer with ½ cup warm water until well mixed.
3 Take the frozen fish blocks one at a time, toss in the potato starch, then dip in the egg replacer and then in the rice crumbs. Fry in a small amount of oil until golden, or bake in the oven for about 20 minutes from frozen. Place any leftovers on a tray to refreeze, then pack in user-friendly packs for future use.

To make these fish fingers you will need a mincer, or you can finely chop the fish and moisten it with a little of the egg replacer.

Serves 2 • Preparation 10 minutes + freezing time • Cooking 20 minutes

Lamb brain patties

2 sets lambs brains
3½ oz/100g superfine flour (page 7)
1 teaspoon gluten-free baking powder
2 cups olive oil

1 Place the brains in a saucepan and cover with cold water. Bring to the boil and simmer for 15 minutes. Drain and place in the refrigerator to cool. Place ¼ cup cold water in a bowl and stir in the flour and baking powder.

2 Heat the oil in a wide, shallow pan. Slice the cold brains into thick slices. Place the slices in the batter and carefully lift with a spoon and place into the hot oil. Cook for a few minutes, then turn and cook the other side. Serve at once.

Serves 2 • Preparation 10 minutes • Cooking 30 minutes

Vegetable pasties

Basic pastry
2 teaspoons gelatine or agar powder
¼ cup olive oil
150g (5oz) flour blend of choice, see
  page 11
½ teaspoon baking soda
2 tablespoons lemon juice

Filling
8 oz/250g vegetables such as carrot,
  turnip, parsnip and potato, diced
2 teaspoons salt
1 tablespoon potato starch
1 cup peas
¼ cup parsley, chopped
1 teaspoon freshly ground black pepper
1 tablespoon margarine, melted
paprika

1 To make the pastry, place ¼ cup cold water in a small saucepan, sprinkle the
   gelatine or agar on top and let stand about 1 minute. Add the oil to the saucepan
   and bring the mixture to the boil, stirring constantly. Remove from the heat and,
   using a wooden spoon, stir in the remaining ingredients until well blended. Fine
   rice flour in a shaker with large holes is useful for rolling if the mixture is a bit
   sticky. This pastry doesn't brown but is cooked after 20 minutes.

2 To make the filling, place the vegetables in a small saucepan with the salt,
   add enough water to cover, bring to the boil, simmer until tender and remove
   vegetables. Reduce the water to about 1 cup and then thicken with the potato
   starch. Add the peas and parsley, set aside to cool and season with pepper.

3 Add the cooked diced vegetables to the sauce. Preheat oven to 400°F/200°C.
   Divide the pastry into four pieces and roll each piece between two sheets of
   plastic. Cut into saucer-size pieces and brush the edges with cold water.

4 Place a spoonful of cooled filling on the pastry and fold over. Press around the
   edges to seal and brush the pastie with a little melted margarine, then sprinkle
   with paprika. Lift carefully onto a paper-lined baking tray and bake for 15 minutes.
   The pasties can be frozen and then reheated.

Serves 2 • Preparation 25 minutes • Cooking 40 minutes

Deep-fried mushrooms

1 egg
1 teaspoon gluten-free baking powder
3½ oz/100g Lola's bread and pastry flour (page 7)
1 teaspoon freshly ground black pepper
1 teaspoon salt
8 oz/250g fresh button mushrooms
2 cups olive oil for frying

1 Whisk together the egg and ¼ cup of cold water. Toss in the flour, baking powder, salt and pepper. Whisk the mixture until it forms a smooth batter. Leave to stand for 5 minutes.

2 Heat the olive oil in a deep saucepan. Dip each mushroom into the batter. Using tongs or a fork, lower the mushrooms, one at a time, into the hot oil. Cook until pale golden, turning if necessary and when cooked drain on kitchen paper.

Serve with green salad and sour cream for a delicious entrée.

Serves 1 • Preparation 15 minutes • Cooking 12 minutes

Spring roll wraps

2 teaspoons salt
2 teaspoons psyllium
7 oz/200g Lola's superfine flour (page 7)
3 tablespoons olive oil

Suggested fillings
lightly cooked minced beef, chicken or pork
shredded Chinese cabbage, sprouts and sliced onion
any Chinese vegetables and chopped prawns (raw egg can be mixed into the
  vegetables)

1 Place 1 cup of warm water, salt and psyllium in a bowl. Using a wire whisk add the
   flour and oil. Leave to stand for 5 minutes. If using a non-stick pan wipe it out with
   a paper towel and a small amount of oil to remove any particles that can cause the
   wraps to stick. Otherwise, you can season a steel frying pan by burning a nob of
   butter in it, wiping clean and regreasing with a little butter. A low to medium heat
   is required to cook the wraps as they should not colour.

2 Heat the pan to a medium heat. Pour about ¼ cup (depending on the size of the
   pan) of mixture in the centre of the pan, lift the pan and roll the mixture around to
   cover the base with a thin layer. Leave to set for about 1 minute, until it will slide
   in the pan. Tip out on a cloth to cool and cover to prevent drying. Continue until
   the mix is used. When cool, store in a plastic bag in the refrigerator until you are
   ready to fill them.

4 To cook the spring rolls, lay the wraps flat and spoon filling onto the centre. Brush
   the edges with a little egg white. Turn in the ends, parcel style and roll up to seal.
   Deep-fry in olive oil for a few minutes until golden.

**Spring rolls can be made in advance and frozen in aluminium foil. Defrost at room
temperature before use.**

Serves 2 • Preparation 20 minutes • Cooking 10 minutes

Spinach fettuccine

½ cup spinach, blanched
1 tablespoon psyllium
1 teaspoon gelatine
3 eggs
1 tablespoon olive oil
10½ oz/300g superfine flour (page 7) plus 55g (2oz) extra for rolling

1 Place ¼ cup water in a bowl and using a blender, process the spinach into the water until there are no visible pieces and you have a green liquid. Add the psyllium and gelatine and let stand for 5 minutes.

2 Add the eggs and oil to a food processor with the softened psyllium and gelatine mix. Blend in 10½ oz/300g of the flour. Turn onto a lightly oiled plastic sheet and knead in the remaining flour. Cover and rest for 1 hour.

3 Divide mixture into four. Commence rolling one part, keeping the other pieces moist in a plastic bag.

4 Using a pasta machine, process the pasta by rolling through the machine. Fold into three, lightly flour the underside and roll again, making sure that the folded edges are at the side of the machine to give a neat edge. Repeat the process 6 times before cutting with the fettuccine cutter of the pasta machine.

5 Wrap the fettuccine loosely around your fingers to form a nest, then refrigerate in a single layer in an airtight container or dry on a tea towel overnight. The pasta can be stored for about 2 weeks in an airtight container when dry.

6 Use plenty of heavily salted water to cook the pasta. Bring to the boil, add the pasta and cook for about 5 minutes. Do not stir. Turn off the heat and leave to stand until the pasta is tender. Lift the pasta carefully with a pasta scoop and top with your favourite sauce.

Serves 2 • Preparation 35 minutes • Cooking 20 minutes

Gnocchi

1 lb/500g sebago potatoes
2 tablespoons gelatine or agar powder
1 teaspoon psyllium
2 egg yolks
pinch of nutmeg
1 teaspoon salt
¾ cup superfine flour (page 7)

1 Boil the potatoes with their skins on. Cool, peel and shred or grate the potato.

2 Place the gelatine or agar, psyllium and egg yolks in 2 tablespoons warm water and whisk slightly to mix, then add nutmeg and salt. Leave to stand 5 minutes. Mix the shredded potato into the mixture and add enough flour to form a soft dough (about ½ cup). Roll into balls using the extra flour, then make a depression with your thumb in each. Set in the refrigerator for at least an hour before cooking.

4 Roll out in a sausage shape, then cut into 30 small pieces. Place the gnocchi in a pot of boiling water and cook for about 10 minutes, until they float. Remove with a draining spoon and serve with your favourite sauce.

Serves 2 • Preparation 35 minutes • Cooking 25 minutes

Fettuccine marinara

Gluten-free fettuccine
1 tablespoon psyllium husks
1 teaspoon gelatine
3 eggs
1 tablespoon olive oil
10½ oz/300g Lola's bread and pastry flour
 (page 7)

Marinara sauce
4 mussels in shell

2 fillets white fish, approximately
 7 oz/200g, cut into pieces
4 oz/125g prawns
4 oz/125g scallops
3 sauce blocks (page 9)
small bunch green onions, chopped
1 stick celery, diced
salt and paprika to taste
few sprigs dill

1 To make the pasta, place ¼ cup of water in a bowl and add the psyllium and gelatine. Add the eggs and oil to a food processor with the softened psyllium and gelatine mix. Blend in 10½ oz/300g of the flour. Turn onto a lightly oiled plastic sheet and knead in the remaining flour. Cover and rest for 1 hour. Divide the mixture into four; commence rolling one part, keeping the other pieces moist in a plastic bag.

2 Using a pasta machine, process the pastry by rolling through the machine. Fold into three, lightly flour the underside and roll again, making sure that the folded edges are at the side of the machine to give a neat edge. Repeat the process six times before making shapes. Dry the finished pasta on a clean tea towel overnight to store for a few weeks or keep in the refrigerator to cook in the next few days. Cook the pasta as directed on page 16 and place in a large serving dish. Scrub the mussel shells and toss them for a few minutes in a pan to open.

3 To make the sauce, place the white fish, prawns and scallops in a saucepan with 2 cups of cold water and bring to simmer point. Turn off the heat and let stand for a few minutes to finish cooking. Remove the seafood and set aside. Add the sauce blocks to the hot fish stock and, when melted, return the mixture to the heat and stir until thickened; stir in the vegetables and add seasoning and some dill if desired. Combine the fish, scallops, prawns and mussels with the sauce and pour over the pasta. When ready to serve, cover the dish and warm for a few minutes in the oven.

Serves 4 • Preparation 35 minutes • Cooking 30 minutes

Beef and bean soup with dumplings

1 lb/500g gravy beef, cut into 3cm cubes
3 large potatoes, cut into 3cm cubes
3 large onions, coarsely chopped
2 large carrots, cut crosswise into 2cm rounds
14 oz/400g canned peeled tomatoes
1 large turnip, coarsely diced
2 celery sticks, coarsely chopped
2 or 3 sauce blocks (page 9)
2 cups spinach leaves, shredded
400g canned mixed beans
salt and freshly ground black pepper

Dumplings
1 tablespoon psyllium
1 egg
1 tablespoon olive oil
10½ oz/100g Lola's bread and pastry flour (page 7)
2 teaspoon gluten-free baking powder
½ teaspoon salt

1 Combine the meat, potatoes, onions, carrots, tomatoes, turnip and celery in a large saucepan. Cover with cold water and simmer for 1 hour.

2 To make the dumplings, sprinkle the psyllium on 2 tablespoons cold water and leave for a few minutes to gel. Whisk the egg and combine with the oil, flour, baking powder, salt and then the psyllium mix.

3 Use a tablespoon to form 6–8cm round dumplings and add to the boiling soup for 1 hour. Remove and test the dumplings – if they are still doughy cook for another 15 minutes and test again. When done, remove the dumplings and thicken the soup with one or two sauce blocks to your desired consistency, stir in the spinach leaves and the beans and season with salt and pepper. Serve with dumplings.

Serves 4 • Preparation 35 minutes • Cooking 2 hours

Plait of perch with lime sauce

1 lb/500g perch fillets
2 teaspoons salt
¼ teaspoon turmeric
2 sauce blocks (page 9)
juice of 2 limes

1   Preheat oven to 360°F/180°C. Divide the fish into four and cut each portion into 3 long, thin pieces. Select 3 strips and secure at one end with a toothpick. Plait the fish, being careful to lay any dark coloured pieces on the underside of the plait. Secure the end of the plait with another toothpick.

2   Place the plaited fish on a greased oven tray, tucking the tail under. Mix half the salt and turmeric and sprinkle over the fish. Bake for approximately 15 minutes.

3   Meanwhile, prepare the lime sauce. Place 1 cup boiling water in a saucepan with the remaining salt and turmeric. Add the sauce blocks and let stand until they melt. Place on heat and whisk until thickened. Stir in the lime juice and adjust flavour by adding more salt if desired.

4   Serve the fish on rice with the lime sauce drizzled on top.

You can use any boneless white fish for this dish.

Serves 2 • Preparation 20 minutes • Cooking 20 minutes

Asian drumsticks with fried rice

juice of 1 lemon
1 tablespoon brown sugar
1 teaspoon salt
3 large chicken drumsticks
1 tablespoon oil
3½ oz/100g rice
6 green beans, sliced in small pieces
1 small carrot, grated
2 sprigs oregano, leaves removed and finely chopped
Asian dipping sauce (page 249)

1 Mix together the lemon juice, brown sugar and salt. Coat the drumsticks with this marinade and stand for 1 hour. Lightly oil a heavy pan and brown the marinated drumsticks until golden. Remove from pan and cook for 15 minutes on high in a covered dish in the microwave.

2 Meanwhile, place oil in a saucepan and add the rice. Stir over heat until the rice is nutty brown. Add 1 cup water and tightly lid the saucepan. Simmer for 6 minutes.

3 Remove from the heat and set aside, still covered while you prepare the vegetables. Combine the rice, beans, carrot and oregano, then season with salt and pepper. Coat the chicken with Asian dipping sauce and arrange on the rice.

Serves 3 • Preparation 75 minutes • Cooking 20 minutes

Seasoned chicken pizza

1 teaspoon salt
1 teaspoon sugar
1 teaspoon agar powder
3 teaspoons dried yeast
5 oz/150g Lola's bread and pastry flour (page 7)

Toppings
7 oz/200g skinless chicken breast fillet
1 red onion, sliced into rings
4 sprigs oregano, leaves removed and finely chopped
12 oven-dried tomatoes
3 tablespoons dairy-free margarine
1 cup rice crumbs
1 teaspoon paprika

1 Preheat the oven to 430°F/220°C. Grease a 12 in/30cm pizza tray with margarine. Place the salt, sugar, agar and yeast in ¾ cup warm water, whisk slightly and stand for 10 minutes. Stir in the flour and whisk well and stand for another 10 minutes. Tip the dough into a jug – it should be pouring consistency (if not, add a little warm water).

3 Pour the mixture onto the greased tray and spread with a spatula to obtain an even, thin coat. Let the mixture stand for 10 minutes while you prepare the chicken pieces.

4 Cut the chicken breast into long thin slices and brown in a hot pan without oil. When the chicken has commenced browning, sprinkle with some water and turn to brown the other side. Do not over-cook the chicken as it will be cooked again in the oven.

5 Place the onion rings and herbs on the pizza dough and place the chicken around in a circle. Decorate with the oven-dried tomatoes. Melt the margarine and add the rice crumbs and paprika. Mix well, then sprinkle over the chicken pieces. Bake for 20–25 minutes.

Serves 2 • Preparation 20 minutes • Cooking 50 minutes

Basic pastry

2 tablespoons gelatine
½ cup/olive oil
10½ oz/300g Lola's bread and pastry flour (page 7)
1 teaspoon bicarbonate of soda
1 teaspoon salt
juice of ½ lemon

1 Sprinkle the gelatine on ½ cup of cold water and leave to soften. Place the gelatine mixture and oil in a large saucepan and heat to dissolve the gelatine. Remove the oil mixture from the heat and sift in the dry ingredients. Add enough lemon juice to form a soft dough.

2 Mix the dough until it forms a ball and will leave the sides of the saucepan. Tip out on to cling wrap and knead through the wrap, lifting and turning until the pastry is smooth. Allow to cool slightly before use. Roll out between two sheets of wrap using a small amount of oil on your hands if necessary.

This pastry is free of dairy products, gluten, wheat, soy and sugar. There is no sugar in this recipe making it perfect for diabetics. In most cases the sweetener can be added to the filling, but if you wish you can add 2 tablespoons of pure icing sugar to the flour. This will make the pastry a little 'sticky' but is good for a slice base that requires little handling. The pastry does not shrink so can be used for blind-baked goods such as tarts.

Serves 2 • Preparation 20 minutes • Cooking 5 minutes

Moussaka

2 large or 4 small eggplants
salt and freshly ground black pepper
1 lb/500g minced lamb
2 cloves garlic, minced
2 onions, finely chopped
¼ cup olive oil
14 oz/400g canned tomatoes
½ bunch oregano, leaves picked and
  chopped

½ cup basil, chopped
½ bunch thyme, leaves picked
½ cup parsley, chopped
2 cups milk
3 sauce blocks (page 9)
3 eggs, lightly whisked
2 oz/60g mozzarella cheese, grated

1 Slice the eggplants in thick slices, sprinkle with salt and set aside. Combine the lamb, garlic, onion, salt and pepper.

2 Use 1 tablespoon of the oil to grease a heavy pan. Brown the meat without stirring – until it smells like barbecued lamb, turn once and brown again for a few minutes. Add the tomatoes, herbs and ½ a cup of cold water. Place in a saucepan and simmer for 15 minutes.

3 Rinse the salt from the eggplants with cold water and dry with paper towel. Place the remainder of the oil in a large frying pan and sauté the eggplant for 5 minutes on each side. Set aside to drain on kitchen paper.

4 Preheat the oven to 320°F/160°C. Heat the milk in a saucepan until boiling, add the sauce blocks and whisk to form a thin sauce. Add the eggs to the custard. Use a large ovenproof casserole dish to bake your moussaka. Pour a thin layer of custard in the bottom of the dish. Arrange a layer of eggplant slices on the custard, then a thick layer of the lamb mixture. Continue to layer the eggplant and meat until it is all used. Pour the custard over the casserole and finish with the mozzarella cheese.

5 Bake for 1 hour, then turn the heat off and leave in the oven until set (about another half hour). Serve with a green salad.

Sauce blocks used in this recipe will prevent the mixture curdling and give a firm texture when serving.

Serves 4 • Preparation 35 minutes • Cooking 95 minutes

Lamb casserole

2 lb/1kg best neck or forequarter lamb chops
2 oz/60g Lola's bread and pastry flour (page 7)
salt and freshly ground black pepper
2 tablespoons olive oil
2 or 3 carrots, quartered crosswise
3 onions, cut in rings
14 oz/400g canned peeled tomatoes
2 potatoes, sliced into 2cm rounds
2 sauce blocks (page 9)

1 Preheat the oven to 360°F/180°C. Trim all excess fat from the lamb chops and toss them in a plastic bag with the flour, salt and pepper. Brown the flour-coated chops in a hot heavy based pan with the oil and then arrange in a covered casserole dish.

2 Surround the chops with the carrots and onions and add the tomatoes and potato slices. Pour 1 cup of water into the frying pan to deglaze the pan, bring to the boil and add the sauce blocks. Whisk to form a thin gravy. Pour the gravy over the casserole. Cover and cook for 1½ hours. Leave to stand for another half hour in the warm oven, or until ready to serve.

This dish can be cooked 1–2 days before you need it. The casserole freezes well.

Serves 4 • Preparation 25 minutes • Cooking 2 hours

Spanish seafood bake

8 oz/250g white boneless fish
4 oz/125g prawns
3–4 sauce blocks (page 9)
salt and freshly ground black pepper
2 sticks celery, diced
1 large onion, diced

Spanish rice topping
1 cup rice
14 oz/400g canned peeled tomatoes
1 tablespoon sugar
1 tablespoon gluten-free curry powder

1 Place the fish and prawns in a large saucepan and cover with cold water, bring to the boil and simmer for 5 minutes. Strain the fish and retain the stock to make the sauce.

2 Thicken the stock with the sauce blocks to make a thick sauce. Season, add the celery, onion, fish and prawns to the sauce. Spoon the fish into a casserole dish.

3 To make the topping, place the rice in a large microwave bowl with the cold water. Microwave on high for 10 minutes and let stand for 10 minutes until the rice is tender and the water has evaporated. Stir with a fork to separate.

4 Mash the canned tomatoes and reduce by cooking over a low heat with the sugar and curry powder for about 15 minutes. Add this mixture to the cooked rice and stir to combine. Pile on top of the seafood mixture. Top with 2 tablespoons melted margarine combined with ¼ cup rice crumbs. Serve with a green salad as a luncheon dish or with vegetables for an evening meal.

Serves 2 • Preparation 25 minutes • Cooking 35 minutes

Seafood chowder served in buns

Buns
1 teaspoon sesame seeds
1 medium potato, peeled and cut into
  2mm cubes
¼ cup olive oil
1 tablespoon gelatine
1 teaspoon sugar
1 teaspoon salt
1 tablespoon dried yeast
8 oz/240g Lola's superfine flour (page 7)
1 oz/30g baby rice flake cereal
1 egg

Seafood chowder
8 oz/250g fillet white fish, sliced
5 oz/150g scallops
4 oz/125g prawns
2 oz/60g butter
10½ oz/100g Lola's superfine flour (page 7)
½ cup white wine
1 teaspoon finely chopped chilli
salt and freshly ground black pepper
1 cup cooked potato, sliced
½ cup chopped celery
½ cup chopped onion

1 To make the buns, preheat oven to 400°F/200°C, grease a large six-hole muffin
   tin and line with sesame seeds. Cook the potato in boiling water for 10 minutes
   and mash with the olive oil. Place the gelatine in 7 oz/200mL of cold water and let
   stand to soften and then heat mixture until clear. Tip the hot gelatine mixture into
   the warm potato and mix well. Add, sugar and salt to this mixture and while it is
   still warm add the yeast. Stand for 5 minutes. Add the remaining ingredients and
   beat for 2 minutes with an electric mixer. Pour the batter into the prepared tins
   and let stand for 10–15 minutes. Cook for about 20 minutes or until they are firm
   and keep warm.

2 Meanwhile, simmer the fish, scallops and shrimps in 3 cups of water until lightly
   cooked. Strain the seafood and return the liquid to a boil. Add the vegetables and
   simmer for 10 minutes. Strain and reserve the liquid as stock. Melt butter in a
   saucepan and stir in the flour. Cook for 1 minute on a low heat. Add the stock and
   wine to the saucepan. Stir the sauce over a low heat until slightly thickened. Add
   the seasonings, vegetables and seafood.

3 Cut a lid off the buns and fill with the chowder. Serve immediately.

Serves 4 • Preparation 50 minutes • Cooking 1 hour

Quiche Lorraine

Pastry
3 oz/80g butter
6 oz/160g Lola's bread and pastry flour (page 7)
1 tablespoon psyllium
1 teaspoon lemon juice

Filling
2 large rashers lean bacon, chopped
2 oz/60g Cheddar cheese, grated
4 eggs
1 cup milk
salt and freshly ground black pepper
½ cup basic sauce (page 246)

1 Blend the pastry ingredients together, adding a little water if necessary to form a soft dough and press into the quiche dish. Chill in the refrigerator for a 30 minutes before adding the filling.

2 Sprinkle the chopped bacon and cheese over the base of the pastry base. Lightly whisk the eggs and milk with the salt and pepper, add the basic sauce and pour over the cheese and bacon (basic sauce here prevents the quiche from curdling if your oven is too hot.) Place the quiche onto a flat tray and freeze for at least an hour or until required. This can be done a day before if necessary.

3 Preheat oven to 320°F/160°C. Place the frozen quiche in the oven for 25 minutes or until firm to touch on the outside of the top. Turn the heat off and leave to stand for a few more minutes until the centre is set – it is important not to overcook the filling. Serve hot with salad or coleslaw.

For a dairy-free quiche, replace the milk with an additional cup of basic sauce (page 246). Cheese can be replaced by corn niblets and the pastry made with the basic pastry recipe (page 80).

Serves 4 • Preparation 35 minutes • Cooking 30 minutes

Curried chicken pies

1 green apple, chopped
1 onion, finely chopped
1 tablespoon olive oil
1 tablespoon gluten-free curry
  powder
1 tablespoon brown sugar
salt and freshly ground black pepper
1 lb/500g lean chicken meat, cut into
  3cm cubes

1 tablespoon potato flour
1 cup coconut milk
2 sauce blocks (page 9)
1 small carrot, diced
1 stick celery, chopped
10½ oz/300g Lola's basic pastry (page 80)

1 Place the apple and onion in a hot pan with the oil. Add the curry powder, brown sugar, salt and pepper, stir over a moderate heat for a few minutes.

2 Toss the chicken pieces into a plastic bag with the potato flour and shake the bag to coat the meat with flour. Add the chicken meat to the curry mixture and stir-fry for a few minutes.

3 Add the coconut milk and bring the mixture to the boil, stirring to prevent burning. Remove from the heat, add the sauce blocks and let stand for a few minutes until the blocks have softened. Return to the heat and stir until the mixture is thick. Add the carrot and celery and simmer for 15 minutes, until the chicken meat is tender.

4 Preheat oven to 360°F/180°C. Roll out half the pastry between two sheets of cling wrap and press into 5 in/12cm pie tins, leaving enough pastry to form the edge of the pie. Roll out the top of the pies and slash to allow steam to escape. Pour the thickened pie meat into the uncooked pastry case.

5 Using a spatula, dip the lid of the pie into a plate of cold water and slide it onto the meat to form the top of the pie. Press with a fork to seal the edges of the pie. Glaze with egg wash or milk. Place in the oven and cook for about 25 minutes or until the base of a pie is crisp and firm to touch.

Makes 4 • Preparation 40 minutes • Cooking 60 minutes

Suet-crushed steak and mushroom pie

Pie filling
1 lb/500g gravy beef, cut into 5cm cubes
2 tablespoons Lola's bread and pastry flour (page 7)
2 tablespoons olive oil
1 onion
4 oz/125g fresh mushrooms
1 teaspoon salt and freshly ground black pepper

Pastry
5 oz/140g finely chopped suet
1 teaspoon salt
11½ oz/330g Lola's bread and pastry flour (page 7)

1 Coat the beef with flour. Place 1 tablespoon olive oil in a hot pan and brown the meat well. Add the onion, mushrooms, salt, pepper and 1 cup of water and simmer with lid on for 1 hour.

2 Add ½ cup cold water to a mixing bowl, stir in the chopped suet, salt and flour and blend with a knife until combined. Turn onto a board and knead for a few minutes. (This can be done in a food processor.) Divide the pastry to line a large basin or pudding bowl, leaving enough to form a lid to cover the filling. Roll out between two sheets of cling wrap and press into basin, making sure that the pastry comes over the edge to form a seal. Suet pastry should be thick as it is quite 'spongy' and light when cooked.

3 Add the filling to the pastry-lined basin then brush the edge with water. Top the pie with the pastry lid, press down the edges and loosely cover with greaseproof paper. Place a wire rack in the bottom of a large saucepan or stockpot and quarter fill with boiling water. Carefully lift the basin into the pan and boil for 2 hours with the lid on.

4 Serve in the basin accompanied by blanched green beans tossed in olive oil and crushed anchovies.

Serves 5 • Preparation 30 minutes • Cooking 3 hours

Meat pies

8 oz/250g finely minced beef
salt and freshly ground black pepper
½ sauce block (page 9)
2½ oz/75g lard
5 oz/150g Lola's bread and pastry flour (page 7)
pinch of turmeric
1 teaspoon salt
juice of ½ lemon
2 tablespoons olive oil
3 tablespoons rice flour

1 Preheat the oven to 400°F/200°C. Brown the meat in a hot pan sprayed with oil. Season with salt and pepper, add 1 cup of water, simmer for a few minutes and thicken with the sauce block. Allow to stand.

2 Place the lard, flour, turmeric, salt, lemon juice and 1 tablespoon of the olive oil in a food processor and blend with the addition of as much ice cold water as necessary to make soft dough. Knead the pastry lightly with some of the rice flour and roll out between two sheets of cling wrap.

3 Cut circles from the pastry to fit your tins (either individual tins or 1 large tin) and smaller circles to go on top. Lift with a spatula to prevent breaking and place the larger circles in the pie tins, pressing into the corners with your fingers.

4 Fill each pie with the meat and top with a smaller circle of pastry that has been dipped in a saucer of cold water to assist with sealing the pie. Slash the top with the point of a sharp knife. (If you wish you can top the pies with mashed potato that has 1 tablespoon of olive oil added to it. Make a ball of the potato and press onto the top of the meat, sealing the edges with a knife.)

5 Brush the tops with the other tablespoon of oil and bake for 20 minutes, or until the base of a pie is crisp and firm to touch.

Serves 2 • Preparation 25 minutes • Cooking 35 minutes

Crab mini quiche

7 oz/200g canned crab meat

Pastry
2 teaspoons gelatine
4 oz/125g butter
8 oz/250g Lola's bread and pastry flour (page 7)

Custard
2 sauce blocks (page 9)
4 eggs, lightly whisked
1 cup milk
salt and freshly ground black pepper
¼ bunch chives, chopped
paprika for sprinkling

1 Preheat oven to 320°F/160°C. Grease 2 in/6cm muffin pan trays. Sprinkle the gelatine on 3 tablespoons of cold water and leave to stand for a few minutes. Chop the butter into blocks and combine all the pastry ingredients to form a firm dough, kneading either, by hand or in a food processor. Cover the pastry while you mix the filling.

2 To make the custard, add the sauce blocks to a cup of boiling water and when they have melted whisk well. Add the eggs, milk, salt, pepper and chives. Place in a jug for pouring into the pans.

3 Divide pastry into four pieces for ease of handling. Roll the pastry between sheets of cling wrap and cut circles with a cookie cutter to fit the pans. Press each circle firmly into the bottom of the pans. Place a small amount of crab meat in the pastry shell and pour the custard over. Sprinkle with paprika. Freeze until ready to cook, or for at least 1 hour. Cook for 30 minutes, or until the custard is set. Serve hot.

Makes 24 • Preparation 30 minutes + freezing time • Cooking 40 minutes

breads & flatbreads

Remember when making bread, that homemade bread is not meant to keep fresh more than one day. The ingredients added to commercial breads to extend shelf-life have chemicals and additional gluten, these are ingredients we want to avoid. You will find that once organised, you will enjoy the challenge of producing fresh, chemical-free foods.

Potato bread

1 tablespoon gelatine
2 oz/60g soft mashed potato
2 oz/60g arrowroot
¼ cup olive oil
1 teaspoon sugar
1 teaspoon salt
1 tablespoon dried yeast
7 oz/200g Lola's bread and pastry flour (page 7)
1 tablespoon baby rice cereal or extra arrowroot
1 egg
2 teaspoons sesame seeds

1 Preheat the oven to 400°F/200°C. Place the gelatine into 7 oz/200mL of cold water and let stand to soften. Select a 9 x 3 x 3 in/23 x 8 x 7cm bread tin to cook the loaf. Bread cooks best in tin, not aluminium.

2 When the gelatine has softened, heat the mixture over low heat until clear. Tip the hot gelatine mixture into the mashed potato and arrowroot and mix well. Add the olive oil, sugar and salt to this mixture and while it is still warm add the yeast.

3 Sift in the flour, baby rice cereal and the beaten egg. Beat the mixture with a rotary beater or whisk. The mixture should be a thick batter – add more warm water if too stiff. Pour the batter into the prepared tin and let it stand for about 15 minutes until bubbles are rising to the surface. Sprinkle with sesame seeds and place in the centre of the oven.

4 Cook for about 40 minutes or until the loaf sounds hollow when tapped.

This mixture is meant to be a quick, easy bread for eating the same day as baked as, all bread once was. If you wish to keep it longer or freeze it, it is necessary to beat it again after the initial 15 minute rise and let it rise again, then beat and leave for another 20 minutes before baking.

Serves 2–4 • Preparation 30 minutes • Cooking 45 minutes

Small white loaf

1 tablespoon dried yeast
1 tablespoon sugar
1 tablespoon gelatine
1 teaspoon salt
1 tablespoon psyllium
½ teaspoon citric acid
10½ oz/300g Lola's superfine flour (page 7)
2 egg whites

1 Grease a 7 x 4 x 3 in/18 x 11 x 10cm bread tin with margarine and line with baking paper. Place ½ cup of hot water and ½ cup of cold, into a medium-sized glass or plastic bowl. Add the yeast, sugar, gelatine, salt and psyllium. Lightly whisk to mix ingredients. Cover the bowl and leave to rise for 15 minutes.

2 Add the flour, citric acid and egg whites to the yeast mixture and mix for 2 minutes, using an electric beater. Cover the bowl with a large plastic bag and leave to rise for 20 minutes. Beat the mixture for 1 minute and scrape into a prepared tin.

3 Preheat oven to 440°F/220°C. Cover the tin with the plastic bag and leave to rise for 25 minutes or less until the mixture is 1 in/25mm from the top of the tin.

4 Bake on the lower shelf for 40 minutes. Remove from oven and wrap in a clean tea towel. Do not cut until cool.

There is no oil in this loaf so it doesn't freeze for long.

Serves 2 • Preparation 50 minutes • Cooking 40 minutes

Hi-top grain loaf

2 tablespoons gelatine
2 teaspoons sugar
2 teaspoons salt
16 oz/450g Lola's superfine flour (page 7)
2 oz/60g brown rice flour
2 tablespoons dried yeast
3 egg whites
2 oz/60g sunflower meal
¼ cup olive oil

1 Grease a heavy 11 x 5 x 4 in/28 x 12 x 10cm bread tin with margarine and line with baking paper. Place 2 cups of cold water into large mixing bowl, add the gelatine, sugar and salt and stand for 2 minutes to soften the gelatine.

2 Heat the gelatine mixture for approximately 1 minute until clear. Add the flour, rice flour and yeast to the warm liquid and beat with an electric mixer for about 1 minute.

3 Cover the bowl with a large plastic bag and leave to rise for 10 minutes. Whisk the egg whites in a separate bowl until stiff. Add the beaten egg whites, sunflower meal and oil to the bread mixture and beat for about 2 minutes.

4 Preheat the oven to 400°F/200°C. Pour the mixture into the prepared tin and leave to rise for 20–25 minutes until about 1 in/25mm from the top of the tin. Bake on the lowest shelf of the oven for 1 hour. Remove from oven and wrap in a clean tea towel. Do not cut until cold.

This loaf freezes well – it is better to slice it before freezing. An electric knife is very good for slicing gluten-free bread. The grainy texture is achieved by the addition of sunflower meal made by blending sunflower kernels for a few minutes.

Serves 2–4 • Preparation 35 minutes • Cooking 1 hour

Sourdough loaf

Starter for sourdough
2 tablespoons dried yeast
6½ oz/180g Lola's superfine flour (page 7)
1 teaspoon sugar
1 teaspoon salt

Bread
4 oz/125mL sourdough starter (see above)
7 oz/200g Lola's superfine flour (page 7)
1 teaspoon salt
1 teaspoon sugar
1 teaspoon dried yeast
1 egg

1 To make the starter for the sourdough, place all starter ingredients, plus 1 cup of lukewarm water in a jar and leave for at least 48 hours. Stir twice daily. Use up to a third of mixture to make sourdough bread. Replace used starter with equal quantities of flour and water and do not use again for another 48 hours.

2 Preheat the oven to 360°F/180°C. To make the bread, select and grease a high loaf tin. Place the starter in a medium-sized bowl add 4 oz/125mL warm water and all the other ingredients. Beat with an electric mixer for 2 minutes. Pour into the greased tin and allow to rise for 30 minutes. Place on a low shelf in the oven and bake for 40 minutes. Cool and refrigerate before slicing.

Its best to use a high loaf tin for this loaf because it has only been allowed to rise once to create a coarse texture. Knocking back after 15 minutes of the first rise and allowing it to rise for 30 minutes again before baking can refine the texture.

Serves 2–4 • Preparation 40 minutes • Cooking 40 minutes

Sandwich bread

2 tablespoons gelatine
3 egg whites
1 teaspoon sugar
2 tablespoons dried yeast
1 teaspoon salt
16 oz/450g Lola's bread and pastry flour (page 7)
2 oz/60g arrowroot
½ cup olive oil

1 Grease a deep loaf tin 11 x 5 x 4 in/28 x 12 x 10cm and line it with baking paper.
   Place the gelatine into 1 cup of the cold water and let it soak until it sinks. Heat the
   gelatine mixture until it is clear. Set aside to cool. Place ½ cup of cold water and ½ cup
   boiling water in a small bowl and add the sugar and yeast. It will become frothy in a
   few minutes.

2 Whisk the egg whites with the salt until stiff. While beating the egg whites, add
   the gelatine mixture a spoonful at a time. Remove from the mixer, sift the flour and
   arrowroot into the egg mixture and fold in the frothy yeast, then the oil.

3 Whisk the mixture to ensure that the ingredients are blended. Cover the basin with
   cling wrap and leave the bread mixture to stand in the basin for about 15 minutes
   until the mixture is puffy – the time is dependent on the quality of the yeast.

4 Preheat the oven to 400°F/200°C. Whisk the dough and repeat the process for a
   second rising. Whisk again and pour into the prepared bread tin. Cover and let
   stand for 20–30 minutes to rise, until it is about an 1 in/2½cm from top of tin – it will
   continue to rise in the oven.

5 Place the bread on the lowest shelf in your oven and after 10 minutes place a scone
   tray on top of the tin to give a square sandwich loaf that is easy to slice. Bake the
   bread for 1 hour. Remove from the oven and cool in the tin before slicing.

Serves 2–4 • Preparation 50 minutes • Cooking 1 hour 10 minutes

Date and linseed loaf

2 tablespoons linseeds
1 teaspoon salt
2 tablespoons caster sugar
2 teaspoons psyllium
2 teaspoons Parisian essence
1 tablespoon liquid glucose
2 teaspoons gelatine
1 tablespoon dried yeast
7 oz/200g Lola's superfine flour (page 7)
1 tablespoon mixed spice
1 tablespoon ground cinnamon
1 tablespoon carob
1 egg
2 tablespoons olive oil
4 oz/125g dates, chopped

1 Grease a 8 in/20cm saddle or log tin with dairy-free margarine and sprinkle with 1 tablespoon of the linseeds. Place ½ cup of cold water in a large glass bowl or microwave dish. Add the salt, caster sugar, psyllium, Parisian essence, liquid glucose and gelatine. Let stand for 1 minute to soften gelatine. Heat the mixture until gelatine dissolves.

2 Stir the yeast into the gelatine mix and whisk slightly. Let stand for 10 minutes. Combine flour, spices, carob and remaining linseeds – dry whisk to blend. Tip the dry ingredients into the yeast mixture. Add the egg and oil and beat with an electric mixer for about 1 minute. Cover and let rise for 20 minutes. Beat again and fold in the chopped dates.

3 Preheat the oven to 360°F/180°C. Spoon into the prepared baking pan, cover and leave again for 20 minutes. Place in the centre of the oven and bake for 30 minutes. Remove from the oven and wrap in a clean tea towel to cool. Serve warm spread with butter.

Serves 2–4 • Preparation 1 hour 5 minutes • Cooking 30 minutes

Brown fruit loaf

16 oz/450g Lola's superfine flour (page 7)
1 teaspoon carob or cocoa
2½ oz/50g sunflower meal
2 teaspoons salt
1 tablespoon treacle
2 tablespoons gelatine

3½ oz/100g pitted prunes
2 tablespoons dried yeast
3 egg whites
2 tablespoons caster sugar
1 teaspoon citric acid
¼ cup olive oil

1 Grease a 11 x 5 x 4 in/28 x 12 x 10cm deep tin well with margarine. Combine the flour, carob and sunflower meal in a plastic bag and shake well. Place 2 cups of cold water, salt, treacle and gelatine in large mixing bowl. Stand for 2 minutes. Chop the prunes in small pieces, dust with a little of the flour to separate.

2 Heat the gelatine mixture in the microwave for 1 minute. Add the flour mixture and yeast to the gelatine mixture and mix well for about 1 minute in an electric mixing machine. Cover the bowl with a large plastic bag. Leave to rise for 10–15 minutes.

3 Preheat the oven to 360°F/180°C. Beat the egg whites in a separate bowl with the caster sugar and citric acid until stiff. Add the beaten egg whites and oil to the bread mixture. Beat the mixture for 2 minutes and pour a thin layer into the prepared tin to coat the bottom of the tin and prevent the fruit sticking to the bottom. Sprinkle the chopped prunes over the batter and add the remaining mixture. Leave to rise for 30 minutes or less, until the mixture is 2½cm from the top of the tin.

4 Bake on lower shelf for 1 hour. Remove from oven and wrap in a clean tea towel to cool.

This bread is not too sweet, can be eaten warm and is good for lunches. The grainy texture is achieved by the blending of sunflower kernels to a meal.

Serves 2–4 • Preparation 35 minutes • Cooking 1 hour

Amaranth wraps

2 tablespoons egg replacer
1 teaspoon salt
5 oz/150g flour blend of choice (page 7)
1 teaspoon gluten-free baking powder
3 tablespoons olive oil
1 tablespoon amaranth cereal

1 Beat the egg replacer, salt (if using) and 1 cup warm water with an electric beater until frothy. Stir in the flour, baking powder and oil.

2 Whisk well until the mixture is a thin smooth batter, then stir in the amaranth cereal. Allow to stand while you prepare the pan. The mixture should be thin enough to pour – if too thick add a little more warm water.

3 Heat the pan to a medium heat and oil lightly. Pour about a cup of the mixture into the pan. Spread well to form a large circle and cook for a few minutes until set. Loosen with a spatula and turn to cook the other side – about 2 minutes. Allow to cool for a minute or two. Remove from pan and cover with foil or place in a plastic bag.

4 Store in the refrigerator and warm before filling to prevent crumbling.

These wraps are cooked in a frying pan, but you can cook them in the oven on a pizza tray or in smaller pans. The amount of mixture should be amended to suit the size of the pan.

Makes 3 wraps • Preparation 25 minutes • Cooking 20 minutes

Yeast-free saddle loaf

1 teaspoon gelatine
2 tablespoons sesame seeds
1 tablespoon glycerine
8 oz/250g Lola's superfine flour (page 7)
3 teaspoons gluten-free baking powder
2 egg whites
½ teaspoon salt
1 tablespoon olive oil

1 Place ¼ cup of cold water in a small bowl and sprinkle the gelatine over it. Let
   stand until the gelatine sinks. Heat the mixture until the gelatine dissolves. Grease
   the bread tin and line it with baking paper or sprinkle with seeds. Place ½ cup
   of warm water into a small bowl with the glycerine. Place the flour and baking
   powder into a large bowl and mix well.

2 Beat the egg whites and salt until stiff. Spoon the warm gelatine mixture into the
   egg whites, a little at a time while beating. Pour the warm glycerine mixture into
   the beaten egg whites, add the dry ingredients and fold the mixture with a large
   wire whisk.

3 Preheat oven to 400°F/200°C. Whisk again and add the oil and an extra 2
   tablespoons of warm water. Check the consistency – it should pour like custard,
   add more water if necessary. Pour into the prepared bread tin and cover with
   plastic wrap. Let stand for 10 minutes. Cook loaf in the centre of the oven for
   40 minutes. Remove from the tin and wrap in a damp cloth until cold.

**This mixture is also good for yeast-free burger buns or a focaccia if cooked in a
slab tin.**

Serves 2–4 • Preparation 25 minutes • Cooking 45 minutes

Pumpkin pan bread

1 teaspoon sugar
2 teaspoons gelatine
1 teaspoon salt
2 teaspoons dried yeast
2 tablespoons warm mashed pumpkin
7 oz/200g flour blend of choice (page 7)
2 tablespoons olive oil

1 Place ½ cup warm water in a medium mixing bowl and add the sugar, gelatine, salt and yeast. Stir in the mashed pumpkin and leave to rise for 10 minutes.

2 Add three-quarters of the flour to the yeast and mix well. Place the remaining flour on a board and tip the dough onto it. Knead lightly until all the flour is absorbed. Oil the basin the bread was mixed in with 1 tablespoon of olive oil.

3 Place the dough back in the bowl and roll it around in the oil to cover the surface. Cover with a cloth and let rest for 20 minutes.

4 Remove dough from the bowl and on a chopping board, form a flat circle of dough to fit the base of your frying pan. If too sticky, use a little fine rice flour and knead into the dough.

5 Oil the pan with the remaining olive oil. Heat your pan to a medium heat and lift the dough and tip it into the pan. Adjust the size if necessary by pressing out a little more with your fingers.

6 Cut the dough into quarters with a knife. Cook the bread for 3 minutes over medium heat before turning with a spatula. Reduce pan heat to low and continue to cook for a further 10 minutes until the bread sounds hollow when tapped.

Cooked in a heavy frying pan, this bread is a quick alternative base for a snack.

Serves 2 • Preparation 30 minutes • Cooking 15 minutes

Bush damper

1 tablespoon psyllium
1 egg
2 teaspoons milk or water for egg wash
7 oz/200g Lola's superfine flour (page 7)
2 tablespoons milk powder
1 tablespoon gluten-free baking powder
1 teaspoon salt

1 Preheat oven to 430°F/220°C. Grease an oven tray or cover with baking paper. Place ¼ cup of cold water in a small bowl and sprinkle the psyllium on top. Whisk lightly and leave to gel for about 3 minutes.

2 To make the egg wash without using an additional egg – lightly whisk the egg in a small mixing bowl. Tip the egg into a large mixing bowl to use in the damper mixture, then add 2 teaspoons of milk or water to the small bowl. Wash around the bowl with the pastry brush and you have egg wash to glaze the damper.

3 To the egg add ¼ cup of warm water and psyllium mix. Place the flour, milk powder, baking powder and salt in a plastic bag and shake well. Add three quarters of the flour mixture to the egg mixture and fold with a table knife to combine into a soft dough. Do not mix more than necessary.

4 Place the remaining flour mixture on a board in a well shape. Tip the soft dough into the well. Knead very quickly a few times to combine all the ingredients. Shape into a damper and mark sections with a knife. Place on the baking tray and glaze with the egg wash. Cook on a high shelf in the oven for about 15 minutes. Remove from the oven and cool on a wire rack covered with a damp tea towel.

Serves 2 • Preparation 25 minutes • Cooking 15 minutes

Seeded country loaf

1 teaspoon gelatine
1 teaspoon sugar
1 tablespoon glycerine
1 tablespoon Parisian essence
1 tablespoon dried yeast
8 oz/250g Lola's superfine flour (page 7)
1 oz/30g sunflower meal
2 egg whites
1 teaspoon salt
2 tablespoons olive oil
3 tablespoons mixed seed such as linseed, sesame or poppy

1 Place ¼ cup of cold water in a small bowl and sprinkle the gelatine over it. Let stand for 1 minute, then heat for 30 seconds to dissolve the gelatine. Grease a 7 x 4 x 3 in/18 x 11 x 8cm loaf pan and line with baking paper. Place the warm water in a bowl with sugar, glycerine, Parisian essence and yeast. Whisk lightly and let stand until frothy, about 10–15 minutes.

2 Combine the flour and sunflower meal. Beat the egg whites and salt until stiff. Spoon the warm gelatine mixture into the egg whites while beating, a little at a time. Pour the frothy yeast mixture into the eggs fold in the dry ingredients with a whisk.

3 Preheat the oven to 400°F/200°C Cover and let stand for 20 minutes. Add the oil to the dough and whisk again with an electric mixer for 1 minute. Fold in seeds and pour into the bread tin. Cover and leave to rise for 30 minutes. Place tin on the middle shelf of the oven and bake for 40 minutes. Remove from the tin, wrap in a clean tea towel and leave to cool before cutting.

Blending sunflower kernels for about 1 minute makes sunflower meal.

Serves 2–4 • Preparation 1 hours 10 minutes • Cooking 40 minutes

Linseed and cheese loaf

2 tablespoons gelatine
¼ cup olive oil
1 teaspoon sugar
1 teaspoon salt
2 tablespoons dried yeast
17½ oz/500g Lola's superfine flour (page 7)
1 tablespoon baby rice flake cereal
2 eggs
2 oz/60g linseeds
4 oz/125g cheddar cheese, grated

1 Preheat the oven to 400°F/200°C. Grease a heavy 11 x 5 x 4 in/28 x 12 x 10cm bread
   tin well with margarine. Line with extra linseeds if desired. Place the gelatine in
   1½ cups of cold water and let stand to soften. When the gelatine has softened heat
   the mixture until clear.

2 Add the olive oil, sugar and salt to this mixture and while it is still warm add
   the yeast. Sift in the flour and baby rice flake cereal. Beat the eggs and add to
   the mixture.

3 Beat with an electric beater for about 1 minute. The mixture should be a thick
   batter. Add a little more warm water if too stiff. Fold in the grated cheese and
   linseeds and pour the batter into the prepared tin. Let it stand for 15 minutes,
   or until mixture is ½ in/1¼ cm from top of tin. It will continue to rise in the oven.
   Cook for about 50 minutes or until the loaf sounds hollow when tapped.

Serves 2–4 • Preparation 30 minutes • Cooking 1 hour

Butternut bread

1 tablespoon gelatine
1 teaspoon sugar
1 teaspoon salt
pumpkin seeds
1 tablespoon dried yeast
8 oz/250g Lola's superfine flour (page 7)
2 egg yolks
½ cup olive oil
2 oz /60g butternut pumpkin, grated

1 Preheat the oven to 400°F/200°C. Place the gelatine, sugar and salt into 7 oz/200mL of cold water and let stand for about 2 minutes to soften the gelatine. Grease a ribbed bottom 12 x 3 in/30 x 8cm saddle loaf tin well with margarine and sprinkle with seeds from the pumpkin.

2 When the gelatine has softened heat the mixture for 1 minute and while it is still warm add the yeast. Stand for 10 minutes to puff the yeast. Sift in the flour and egg or egg-replacer mixture. Add the oil and beat the mixture with an electric beater for about 1 minute. The mixture should be a thick batter. Add a little more warm water if too stiff.

3 Pour a thin layer of the batter into the prepared tin and sprinkle about one third of the grated pumpkin over it. Repeat the method until all the batter and pumpkin is used. Leave the mixture to rise in the tin for 10–15 minutes, or until mixture is ½ in/1¼cm from top of tin. It will still continue to rise in the oven.

4 Cook for about 40 minutes or until the loaf sounds hollow when tapped.

This loaf was baked using 2 egg yolks, which can be replaced with 1 egg or equivalent egg replacer.

Serves 2–4 • Preparation 40 minutes • Cooking 40 minutes

Herb and onion bread

1 tablespoon gelatine
1 teaspoon sugar
1 teaspoon salt
1 tablespoon sesame seeds
1 tablespoon dried yeast
8 oz/250g Lola's superfine flour (page 7)
1 egg
½ cup olive oil
1 tablespoon dried onion
1 teaspoon fresh or dried herbs

1 Preheat the oven to 400°F/200°C. Place the gelatine, sugar and salt into 7 oz/200mL of cold water and let stand for about 2 minutes to soften the gelatine. Grease a 12 x 3 in/30 x 8cm saddle tin well with margarine and sprinkle with sesame seeds. When the gelatine has softened heat the mixture for 30 seconds and add the yeast. Stand for 10 minutes to puff the yeast.

2 Sift in the flour. Add the egg and oil and beat the mixture with an electric beater for about 1 minute. The mixture should be a thick batter. Add a little more warm water if too stiff. Fold in the dried onion and herbs and pour into the prepared tin.

3 Leave the mixture to rise in the tin for 10–15 minutes, or until mixture is 1¼ cm from top of tin. It will continue to rise in the oven.

4 Cook for about 40 minutes or until the loaf sounds hollow when tapped.

Serves 2 • Preparation 30 minutes • Cooking 40 minutes

Hamburger buns

2 tablespoons gelatine
2 teaspoons sugar
2 teaspoons salt
17½ oz/500g Lola's superfine flour (page 7)
2 tablespoons dried yeast
3 egg whites
½ teaspoon citric acid
½ cup olive oil

1 Preheat the oven to 400°F/200°C. Grease three heavy pudding trays with margarine. Place 2 cups of cold water into a large mixing bowl and add the gelatine, sugar and salt. Stand for 2 minutes to soften the gelatine. Heat the gelatine mixture for approximately 1 minute until clear. Add the flour and yeast to the warm liquid and beat with an electric mixer for about 1 minute.

2 Cover the bowl with a large plastic bag. Leave to rise for 10 minutes. Whisk the egg whites and citric acid in a separate bowl until stiff. Add the beaten egg whites and oil to the bread mixture and beat for about 2 minutes.

3 Pour the mixture into the prepared pans and leave to rise for 10–15 minutes until they are puffy. Bake on the middle shelf of the oven for 15 minutes. Remove from oven and wrap in a clean tea towel. Do not cut until cold.

Serves 2–4 • Preparation 40 minutes • Cooking 15 minutes

Poppy seed plaits

3 tablespoons poppy seeds, plus 1 extra tablespoon for the tin
1 tablespoon gelatine
2 teaspoons salt
2 teaspoons sugar
4 oz/125g warm mashed potato
¼ cup olive oil
2 tablespoons dried yeast
17½ oz/500g Lola's superfine flour (page 7)
2 eggs

1 Preheat the oven to 400°F/200°C. Grease a four-loaf plait bread tin well with margarine. Line with the extra poppy seeds. Place the gelatine, salt and sugar in 2 cups of cold water and let stand for 2 minutes.

2 When the gelatine has softened heat the mixture until clear. Tip the hot gelatine mixture into the mashed potato and mix well. Add the olive oil to this mixture and while it is still warm add the yeast. Sift in the flour. Beat the eggs and add to the mixture.

3 Beat the mixture with an electric beater for about 1 minute. The mixture should be a thick batter. Add a little more warm water if too stiff. Fold the seeds into the mixture. Pour the batter into the prepared tin. Let it stand for 10–15 minutes or until mixture is puffy. It will continue to rise in the oven. Cook for about 20 minutes or until the loaves sound hollow when tapped.

Serves 2–4 • Preparation 25 minutes • Cooking 20 minutes

Bacon bread ring

1 teaspoon salt
1 teaspoon sugar
2 teaspoons psyllium
2 teaspoons gelatine
1 tablespoon dried yeast
1 egg white
½ teaspoon citric acid
¼ cup olive oil
8 oz/250g Lola's superfine flour (page 7)
4 oz/125g bacon pieces

1 Grease a 3 x 8 in/8 x 20cm ring pan with margarine. Remove the mixture from microwave. Place the slat, sugar, psyllium and gelatine in 1 cup of cold water and let stand for 2 minutes. When the gelatine has softened heat until dissolved.

2 Stir the yeast into the gelatine mix and whisk slightly. Let stand for 10 minutes. Beat the egg white and citric acid until stiff, and add to yeast mixture with the oil and flour. Using an electric mixer beat well for about 2 minutes. Cover and let rise for 10 minutes. Whisk for 1 minute. Fold in the chopped bacon pieces.

3 Preheat the oven to 360°F/180°C. Spoon into the prepared baking pan, cover and leave again for 20 minutes to rise. Place pan in the centre of the oven and bake for 40 minutes. Remove from the oven and wrap in a clean tea towel to cool.

For a low-fat option, the bacon pieces can be grilled to remove fat if desired or you can add them raw and decrease the oil to 2 tablespoons, plus 2 tablespoons of warm water.

Serves 2 • Preparation 45 minutes • Cooking 40 minutes

Baps

1 teaspoon sugar
1 tablespoon gelatine
1 tablespoon dried yeast
2 egg whites
1 teaspoon salt
½ teaspoon citric acid
8 oz/250g Lola's superfine flour (page 7)
2 tablespoons olive oil

1 Grease a Yorkshire pudding tray with some dairy-free margarine. Place the sugar and gelatine in 1 cup of cold water and let stand for 1 minute to soften, or until the liquid is clear. Add the yeast and stand for 10 minutes.

2 Whisk the eggs, salt and citric acid in a separate bowl with an electric mixer until stiff. Tip the flour into the yeast mixture. Beat in the oil and whisked eggs for 1 minute with electric mixer. Cover and let stand again for 10 minutes.

3 Preheat the oven to 360°F/180°C. Spoon the mixture into the tins and leave until puffy – about 15 minutes. Dust the tops with sifted flour. Place in the centre of the oven and bake for 10 minutes.

4 Remove from the oven and wrap in a clean tea towel to cool then place in a plastic bag until ready to serve.

These soft-topped rolls were baked in Yorkshire pudding trays. They are served fresh from the oven for breakfast in Scotland.

Serves 2–4 • Preparation 35 minutes • Cooking 10 minutes

Black bread

2 tablespoons poppy seeds for lining tin
1 teaspoon salt
¼ cup molasses
1 tablespoon dried yeast
6 oz/160g Lola's superfine flour (page 7)
3 oz/90g sunflower meal
1 tablespoon carob
1 tablespoon psyllium
3½ oz/100g brown rice flour
1 egg
¼ cup olive oil
1 teaspoon Parisian essence
1 tablespoon caraway seeds

1 Grease a small bowl-shaped tin with some margarine and line it with poppy seeds. Add the salt, molasses and yeast to 1 cup of warm water and stand 10 minutes.

2 Combine the flour, sunflower meal, carob, psyllium and rice flour. Add half the flour mixture to the yeast and whisk in the egg and oil then beat in the remaining flour and Parisian essence with an electric mixer. Cover and let stand again for 15 minutes.

3 Preheat the oven to 360°F/180°C. Whisk the bread mixture, add the caraway seeds, pour into the seeded tin and leave to rise for about 20 minutes. Place in the middle of the oven and bake for about 40 minutes. Remove from the oven and cool in the tin. Wrap in a clean tea towel and refrigerate overnight before cutting.

This gluten-free version of traditional Hungarian black bread is baked in a bowl-shaped tin that is lined with poppy seeds. Blending sunflower kernels for a few minutes in the blender makes sunflower meal.

Serves 2–4 • Preparation 1 hour 30 minutes • Cooking 40 minutes

Challah plait

1 tablespoon gelatine
3 tablespoons sesame seeds
2 tablespoons dried yeast
3 egg whites
2 tablespoons sugar
2 teaspoons salt
1 teaspoon citric acid
17½ oz/500g Lola's superfine flour (page 7)
3 tablespoons olive oil

1 Grease a plait-patterned or ring tin with margarine and sprinkle with the sesame seeds. Place 2 cups of cold water into a large glass bowl or microwave dish. Add gelatine and let stand for 1 minute to soften. Heat the gelatine mixture for 50 seconds or until gelatine is dissolved.

2 Add the yeast and stand for 10 minutes. Whisk the eggs, sugar, salt and citric acid in a separate bowl, with an electric mixer until stiff.

3 Tip the flour into the wet mixture. Beat in the oil and whisked eggs for 1 minute with electric mixer. Cover the basin and let stand again for 10 minutes.

4 Preheat the oven to 400°F/200°C. Whisk again and pour the mixture into the tin and leave for about 20 minutes to rise Place in the centre of the oven and bake for 45 minutes. Remove from the oven and wrap in a clean tea towel to cool then place in a plastic bag until ready to serve.

Pronounced (Hallah), this Israeli plaited soft bread with a golden colour and seeded top is used as Friday night bread by the Jewish community. For New Year it is baked with sultanas, in round loaves, to represent the roundness of the year. At the evening meal it is customary to eat symbolic foods.

Serves 2–4 • Preparation 40 minutes • Cooking 45 minutes

Naan flats

½ cup milk
1 teaspoon sugar
1 teaspoon salt
1 teaspoon gelatine
1 tablespoon dried yeast
8 oz/250g Lolas superfine flour (page 7)
1 teaspoon bicarbonate of soda
2 tablespoons olive oil

1 Place the milk in a glass or china bowl. Add the sugar, salt and sprinkle on the gelatine, leave to stand for 1 minute. Heat for one minute or until sugar is dissolved and add the yeast to the warm milk. Stand for 10 minutes.

2 Cut four tear-shaped ovals about 8 x 6 in/21 x 16cm of heavy baking paper or foil. Preheat a flat oven tray under a hot griller. Add the flour, bicarbonate of soda and oil to the yeast mixture and mix well to form a light dough.

3 Tip out on a board and knead lightly using a little more flour if necessary. Be careful not to add too much extra flour, as this will dry your breads. Heat the griller to its highest temperature.

4 Divide dough into four pieces and press out on the shaped papers. Cover with a cloth and leave to stand for 10 minutes. Brush the breads with cold water and place under the hot griller for 3–4 minutes until bubbled and brown. Remove, stack and cover with a cloth to prevent drying. Repeat, if necessary.

This method will allow you to produce a reasonable gluten-free version of naan bread. Grilled on ovals of baking paper on a preheated oven tray it is served hot with traditional Indian dishes such as tandoori chicken.

Serves 2–4 • Preparation 25 minutes • Cooking 12 minutes

Herb focaccia

1 teaspoon gelatine
pinch salt
1 teaspoon sugar
1 tablespoon dried yeast
¼ cup olive oil
5 oz/140g Lola's superfine flour (page 7)
1 egg or egg substitute
1 teaspoon mixed herbs
1 teaspoon sesame seeds

1 Grease the sides of a round bread pan and cut a circle of baking paper to line the bottom. Add the gelatine, salt and sugar to ½ cup cold water and leave to stand for 1 minute. Heat the mix until the gelatine dissolves. Add the yeast and stand for 10 minutes.

2 Using an electric mixer beat in the oil, flour and egg for about 1 minute to make sure the yeast is well distributed. Stir in the mixed herbs.

3 Preheat the oven to 440°F/220°C. Pour the batter into one or two prepared tins and leave the mixture to stand for 20 minutes until bubbles form – it does not rise much in the tin.

4 Sprinkle the top with sesame seeds and cook for 10–20 minutes depending on thickness.

This mixture can be baked in one or two 8 in/20cm round sponge tins depending on the thickness of the bread required. It contains no gluten, wheat, corn or egg (if egg substitute is used).

Serves 2 • Preparation 20 minutes • Cooking 20 minutes

Irish griddle bread

2 tablespoons milk, warmed
1 teaspoon sugar
2 tablespoons baby rice cereal
7 oz/200g Lola's superfine flour (page 7)
2 teaspoons gluten-free baking powder
2 tablespoons olive oil

1   Place the warm milk in a medium mixing bowl and add the sugar, baby rice cereal, three quarters of the flour and the baking powder. Mix well with a knife. Place the remaining flour on a board and tip the bread mix onto it. Knead lightly until all the flour is absorbed.

2   Oil the basin the bread was mixed in with 1 tablespoon of olive oil. Place the dough back in the bowl and roll it around in the oiled basin to cover the surface with oil. Cover with a cloth and let rest for 10 minutes.

3   Remove dough from the bowl and flatten on a board to form a circle to fit the base of your pan. If too sticky use a little fine rice flour to press out the dough.

4   Oil a heavy frying pan and heat to a medium heat. Using the board to lift the dough, tip it into the pan. Adjust the size if necessary by pressing out a little more with your fingers. Cut the dough into four quarters with a knife. Cook the bread for 3 minutes on the medium heat before turning with a spatula. Reduce the pan heat to low and continue to cook for a further 10 minutes until the bread sounds hollow when tapped.

Serves 1–2 • Preparation 25 minutes • Cooking 15 minutes

Choux cheese bread

1 teaspoon salt
5 oz/130g butter
8 oz/250g Lola's superfine flour (page 7)
5 eggs
8 oz/250g Gruyère cheese, cubed
1 oz/30g Cheddar cheese, grated

1 Preheat oven to 400°F/200°C. Cover a large oven tray with silicone baking paper. Place 1½ cups of water, salt and butter in a saucepan and bring the boil. When boiling add all the flour and combine with a wooden spoon. Cook, stirring until mixture leaves the side of pan.

2 When cool add the eggs one at a time, stirring briskly with wooden spoon. Add the Gruyère cubes to the pastry and mix well.

3 Heap the mixture like a cake, onto the centre of the baking tray. Sprinkle with the grated cheddar cheese. Cook for 1 hour.

Serves 2–4 • Preparation 15 minutes • Cooking 60 minutes

Panettone

1 tablespoon dried yeast
3½ oz/100g sugar
7 oz/200g Lola's superfine flour (page 7)
2 eggs separated
½ teaspoon salt
2 oz/60g softened butter
2 teaspoons vanilla essence
4 oz/125g sultanas
2 oz/60g mixed peel

1 Grease a deep tin with margarine. Dissolve yeast in ½ cup of warm water with 1 tablespoon of the sugar and half the flour. Mix well, cover and allow to rise until puffy – about 20 minutes.

2 Beat egg whites, salt and remaining sugar until stiff and add to the dough, alternating with remainder of the flour.

3 Add egg yolks and softened butter then beat with electric mixer for 2 minutes. Cover and let mixture rise again until doubled, about 20 minutes. Punch down and add the vanilla essence.

4 Preheat the oven to 320°F/160°C. Pour a little mixture into tin, add sultanas and peel then more mixture, continuing this method until all the fruit and mixture is used. Allow mixture to stand for about 30 minutes or until the tin is three-parts full. Cook for 40 minutes on low shelf.

Cooked in a traditional tall tin this Italian yeast cake is served with breakfast coffee throughout the year and is used for gift-giving at Christmas. You can make smaller versions by using large fruit cans.

Serves 2–4 • Preparation 1 hour 15 minutes • Cooking 40 minutes

Pumpernickel

2 oz/60g fine polenta
1 teaspoon salt
¼ cup molasses
¼ cup olive oil
3½ oz/100g Lola's superfine flour (page 7)
2 oz/60g brown rice flour
1 tablespoon dried yeast
1 egg
1 tablespoon carob
1 teaspoon Parisian essence
1 tablespoon caraway seeds

1 Grease a small bread tin with some margarine and line it with silicone baking paper. Place 1½ cups of boiling water in a saucepan over high heat and slowly whisk the polenta into the rapidly boiling water. Cook for a few minutes until smooth. Add the salt, molasses and oil and leave to cool slightly.

2 Add half the flour, brown rice flour and the yeast to the warm mixture and stand for 15 minutes. Whisk in the egg, remaining flour, carob and Parisian essence with an electric mixer. Stir in caraway seeds. Cover and let stand again for 15 minutes.

3 Preheat the oven to 300°F/150°C. Place a large tin half-full of hot water in the oven. Pour the bread mixture into a 7 x 4 x 4 in/18 x 11 x 10cm tin and leave for about 30 minutes to rise. Place the small tin in the water bath and cook for 2 hours. Remove from the oven and cool in the tin. Wrap in a clean tea towel and refrigerate overnight before cutting.

Serves 2–4 • Preparation 1 hour 10 minutes • Cooking 2 hours

Pita bread

1 teaspoon gelatine
2 teaspoons psyllium
1 tablespoon dried yeast
1 teaspoon salt
1 teaspoon sugar
2 tablespoons olive oil
7 oz/200g Lola's superfine flour (page 7)

1 Place 2 ceramic tiles in the oven and preheat to 440°F/220°C. Cut four oval-shaped pieces of baking paper about 9 in/22cm long. Add the gelatine and psyllium to ½ cup of cold water and let stand for 1 minute to soften

2 Heat the gelatine mix until gelatine dissolves. Add the yeast, sugar and salt to the warm water. Leave to stand 10 minutes until puffy. Add half the flour and mix well with a knife.

3 Tip the oil on the dough and knead using a heavy plastic spatula or wooden spoon. Continue kneading for about 5 minutes until the oil is absorbed. Cover and leave to stand 10 minutes. Turn onto a lightly floured board and knead for 5 minutes using the remainder of the flour. Divide dough into four teardrop shapes.

4 Press dough out on the oval paper using the board and a few drops of oil. Cover the ovals with a cloth to rise for 20 minutes. Using a metal spatula or egg slice to lift the pita, place dough on hot tiles, brush with oil and cook for 3 minutes, lower heat to 400°F/200°C and leave for another 1 minute until puffed and slightly golden. These breads are meant to be chewy and moist. Cool in a plastic bag to prevent drying.

These pita breads are cooked on ceramic glazed tiles on the oven wire racks. These can be bought at any tile shop — unglazed are best.

Serves 2 • Preparation 45 minutes • Cooking 10 minutes

Barbari pockets

1 teaspoon honey
1 teaspoon gelatine
2 teaspoons psyllium
1 teaspoon salt
1 tablespoon dried yeast
10 oz/300g Lola's superfine flour (page 7)

1 teaspoon paprika
½ teaspoon cayenne pepper
3 tablespoons olive oil
¼ cup fine rice flour for rolling

1 Place a heavy flat oven tray in the oven and preheat to 360°F/180°C.

2 Cut 4 x 6 in/15cm circles of baking paper. Place 7 oz/200mL of warm water in a bowl and add the honey, gelatine, psyllium, salt and yeast. Stir with a fork, cover and leave to stand for 5 minutes.

3 Add half the flour to the yeast mixture. Cover and stand to rise for 10 minutes. Add the remainder of the flour, spices and oil. Mix well with a knife using a cutting action and tip onto a board.

4 Knead for a few minutes until smooth, using the rice flour if necessary. Divide the dough into four balls. Press out half a ball on each paper, using your fingers with a little rice flour if necessary. Cover remaining dough with a cloth to prevent drying. Place circles on the baking tray. Press out matching circles of dough, using oil to assist.

5 Brush halfway around the bottom circle with water to stick the top and leave an opening. Top the bottom dough portions with the 'lid' and peel back the oiled plastic to use again to make the next lid.

6 Cover the prepared pockets with a cloth and leave to stand about for 20 minutes. Brush with a little oil. Cook for 5 minutes in the preheated oven, then reduce the heat and cook for another 3 minutes. Remove from the oven and wrap in a cloth and place in a plastic bag to cool. Baking paper circles can be reused next time.

This Persian bread is ideal filled with salad for lunches. Fine rice flour in a sprinkler canister is useful for all gluten free pastry rolling.

Serves 2 • Preparation 40 minutes • Cooking 10 minutes

cakes, buns & cookies

Many enterprising home bakers have started businesses baking gluten free biscuits, cakes etc, which is great news if you know where they are located. In addition some home based companies are now producing ready-to-bake bread, muffins and biscuit mixes. However, with this book you will able to make your own with the best of them!

Basic bun dough

1 tablespoon gelatine
1 tablespoon psyllium
2 tablespoons sugar
1 teaspoon salt
2 tablespoons glycerine
1 tablespoon dried yeast
16 oz/450g Lola's superfine flour (page 7)
1 egg
1 tablespoon mixed spice (optional)
2 tablespoons soft margarine

1 Place 7 oz/200mL of cold water in a microwave bowl and sprinkle the gelatine and psyllium on top. Leave to stand for a few minutes to soften and heat until gelatine dissolves.

2 Remove from heat, add sugar, salt, glycerine and yeast, and stir to mix. Cover and stand for 20 minutes until mixture is doubled. Oil a sheet of plastic about 12 x 9 in/30 x 22cm.

3 Using an electric mixer whisk about three-quarters of the flour into the yeast mixture. Add the egg, spice and margarine and beat until a smooth batter forms.

4 Cover and stand again for 20 minutes, then beat again for 1 minute. Using a spatula fold in the remaining flour and tip onto the plastic sheet. Lightly knead using a little fine rice flour if required. Use as directed.

This easy bun mixture is used to make many different buns. If you find it a little sticky when kneading use a sprinkle of fine rice flour. The dough should be as soft as possible to make a light bun. To make the dough into buns, divide mixture into lightly greased friand tins, allow to rise for 20 minutes and then bake for 30 minutes or until well risen and golden.

Preparation 50 minutes • Cooking as required

Banana cupcakes

1 tablespoon egg replacer
2 teaspoons gelatine or agar powder
1 small banana
2 tablespoons olive oil
3½ oz/100g caster sugar
5 oz/150g flour blend of choice (page 7)
2 teaspoons vanilla essence
2 teaspoons gluten-free baking powder
1 teaspoon baking soda

1 Preheat the oven to 360°F/180°C. Line a cupcake tray with cupcake cases. Place ⅓ cup warm water in a bowl with the egg replacer and gelatine or agar. Let stand while you mash the banana and oil together.

2 Beat the egg replacer mixture until thick. Gradually add the caster sugar and continue beating until the consistency of a thick meringue.

3 Fold in the banana and oil and then the flour, vanilla, baking powder and baking soda, using a wire whisk to produce a cupcake mixture that will hold its shape.

4 Spoon the mixture into the cupcake cases to three-quarter-fill each cup. Bake for 15 minutes.

Serves 2–4 • Preparation 15 minutes • Cooking 15 minutes

Apple and sultana spice ring

1 teaspoon salt
2 tablespoons caster sugar
1 tablespoon gelatine
2 oz/60g mashed potato
1 tablespoon dried yeast
8 oz/250g Lola's superfine flour (page 7)
1 teaspoon ground ginger
1 teaspoon mixed spice

1 teaspoon ground cinnamon
2 eggs
1 cup sultanas
1 medium apple, peeled and chopped

Topping
2 cups pure icing
3 tablespoons margarine
walnuts, to decorate

1 Preheat the oven to 360°F/180°C. Grease an 8 in/20cm ring pan. Place 7 oz/200mL of cold water in a glass bowl. Add the salt, caster sugar and gelatine. Let stand for 1 minute to soften gelatine. Heat the gelatine mixture until clear.

2 Whisk the mashed potato into the warm gelatine mixture. Stir in the yeast and whisk slightly. Let stand for 3 minutes. Combine flour and spices. Lightly whisk the eggs with an electric mixer.

3 Tip the dry ingredients into the yeast mixture and beat in the eggs. Beat the mixture for 1 minute with the electric mixer. Pour a quarter of the mixture into the pan and spread over the base. Sprinkle a quarter of the sultanas and apple over the mixture and top with more batter.

4 Sprinkle over the remaining fruit and cover with more mixture. Leave to stand for 15 minutes until a few bubbles appear. Place in the centre of the oven and bake for 35 minutes. Remove from the oven and wrap in a clean tea towel to cool.

5 Cream together icing sugar and margarine, adding a little hot water if necessary. Ice the cake when cool, and decorate with walnuts.

One medium-sized potato produces approximately 2 oz/60g mashed potato.

Serves 4–6 • Preparation 30 minutes • Cooking 35 minutes

Currant and custard scrolls

1 batch of basic bun dough (page 162)
½ cup currants

Custard
2 tablespoons margarine
2 tablespoons Lola's superfine flour (page 7)
1 egg yolk
½ cup sugar
vanilla essence
3 tablespoons almond meal

Bun glaze
1 teaspoon gelatine
2 tablespoons sugar

3 To make the custard, melt the margarine in a small saucepan and add the flour. Cook for 1 minute stirring with a wooden spoon. Add ½ cup of boiling water and cook until the custard is thick. Add the egg yolk, sugar, vanilla and almond meal, and stir well. It should be thick enough to hold its shape, if not add a little more almond meal.

2 Preheat the oven to 360°F/180°C. Oil a sheet of cling wrap about 12 x 9 in/30 x 22cm. Cover a baking tray with silicone baking paper. Press the dough out on the cling wrap. Spread with the custard filling, and sprinkle with currants.

2 Roll the dough up lengthwise using the cling wrap to help. Using an oiled knife, cut the scrolls in thick slices and place on the prepared tray. Leave the scrolls to rise for 20 minutes. Bake for 15 minutes.

4 To make the bun glaze, boil ingredients together with 2 tablespoon of water. Remove buns from oven and brush with glaze while still hot.

Serves 2–4 • Preparation 35 minutes • Cooking 20 minutes

Hi-fibre carrot slice

7 oz/200g Lola's all-purpose flour (page 7)
2 teaspoons gluten-free baking powder
1 tablespoons gelatine
1 tablespoon psyllium
2 teaspoons mixed spice
2 oz/60g desiccated coconut
4 oz/125g finely grated carrot
4 oz/125g sultanas
6 oz/170g brown sugar
½ cup olive oil
2 teaspoons vanilla essence
3 eggs

Lemon frosting
8 oz/250g sifted pure icing sugar
1 tablespoon butter
1 tablespoon lemon juice

1 Preheat the oven to 360°F/180°C. Grease a 10 x 7 x 2 in/26 x 18 x 5cm baking tin and line the bottom with baking paper. Lightly whisk the eggs.

2 Combine the flour, baking powder, gelatine, psyllium, spices, coconut, carrot and sultanas. Place the brown sugar, oil and vanilla essence in a large saucepan and warm slightly. Remove from the heat and add all the other ingredients, alternating the dry ingredients with the eggs. Combine well and spoon into the baking tin.

3 Bake the centre shelf of the oven for 25 minutes. Leave to cool in the tin. When cold, ice with lemon frosting.

4 To make the lemon frosting, whisk ingredients together well and use to top the cooled cake.

Serves 2–4 • Preparation 20 minutes • Cooking 25 minutes

Oven-baked doughnuts

⅓ cup rice milk
2 teaspoons gelatine or agar powder
¼ teaspoon salt
1 teaspoon sugar
1 tablespoon dried yeast
3 egg whites
2 teaspoons vanilla essence
5 oz/150g pure icing sugar
4½ oz/130g superfine flour (page 7)
2 oz/60g margarine, melted

1 Preheat the oven to 320°F/160°C. Grease a non-stick doughnut tray with margarine. Place the milk in a bowl, add the gelatine or agar, salt and sugar, then heat until clear.

2 Stir in the dried yeast, then set aside to rise for a few minutes while you whisk the eggs, vanilla and icing sugar to a stiff meringue.

3 Add the yeast mixture to the meringue. Using a wire whisk, blend in the flour and melted margarine.

4 Spoon into the greased doughnut cups. Leave to stand for 15 minutes, then bake for 12 minutes. Finish with cinnamon or icing sugar as desired.

These doughnuts freeze well.

Serves 2–4 • Preparation 25 minutes • Cooking 12 minutes

Strawberry shortcake

4 eggs
3½ oz/100g caster sugar
2 teaspoons margarine
1 tablespoon glycerine
3½ oz/100g Lola's bread and pastry flour (page 7)
2 teaspoons gluten-free baking powder
2 teaspoons vanilla essence
pure icing sugar to dust

Filling
5 oz/150g fresh strawberries
1 cup fresh cream, whipped

1 Preheat the oven to 360°F/180°C. Grease the sides and line the bottom of 2 x 8 in/20cm round cake tins with baking paper. Place the eggs and caster sugar in a large metal bowl and hand whisk over a saucepan of hot water until the mixture is slightly warm and frothy.

2 Remove from the heat and continue beating with a rotary or electric mixer until the mixture is thick and creamy but not stiff. Add the margarine and glycerine to 4 tablespoons of hot water and let stand for 1 minute.

3 Fold in the sifted flours and baking powder to the beaten eggs and sugar. Mix in the vanilla essence, glycerine mix. Fold lightly but thoroughly.

4 Pour into the prepared tins, level quickly with a plastic spatula and cook for 30 minutes. Let stand in the tin for 1 minute before turning onto a wire rack to cool. When the cakes are cold, select 8 small strawberries for decoration and set aside.

5 Slice the remaining strawberries into the whipped cream and fold through. Sandwich the cream mix between the two cakes. Pipe 8 rosettes of the whipped cream in a circle on top of the shortcake, place a berry on each rosette. Dust the top of the shortcake with pure icing sugar.

Serves 2–4 • Preparation 45 minutes • Cooking 30 minutes

Passionfruit sponge

4 eggs
5 oz/150g caster sugar
5 oz/150g Lola's all-purpose flour (page 7)
4 teaspoons gluten-free baking powder
1 tablespoon margarine

Passionfruit icing
2 tablespoons pure icing sugar, sieved
1 tablespoon margarine
2 passionfruit, pulped scooped out

1 Preheat the oven 360°F/180°C. Grease the sides of 2 x 8 in/20cm flan tins and dust
   with gluten-free flour mixture. Line the bottom with baking paper. Do not use
   aluminium pans as your sponge will not cook evenly; it will cook at the edges before
   the centre, giving you a dry result.

2 Hand whisk the eggs and caster sugar over hot water until they are just warm and
   bubbly. Using an electric mixer, beat until the mixture is thick and creamy. Sift the
   flour and baking powder and fold into the egg mixture. Add the margarine to
   3 tablespoons of boiling water and when melted pour the mixture down the inside
   of the bowl.

3 Fold the mixture with a wire whisk, being careful not to over mix as this will release
   the air and flatten the sponge. Pour into the tin and gently move the mixture with
   a spatula so that a small depression is made in the centre of the cake. Place in the
   centre of the preheated oven and cook for 15 minutes. Turn off the oven and stand
   for 5 minutes in the oven before removing and turning out.

4 To make the passionfruit icing, combine the icing ingredients with 1 tablespoon of
   boiling water and pour on the top of one cake. Fill the cake with whipped cream,
   softened creamed ricotta cheese or patisserie custard.

Unfilled cakes freeze well if foil-wrapped. They will dry if only plastic-wrapped.

Serves 2–4 • Preparation 30 minutes • Cooking 20 minutes

Orange poppy seed log

3 eggs
5 oz/150g caster sugar
5 oz/150g Lola's all-purpose flour (page 7)
3 oz/90g ground almonds
grated zest of 2 oranges
2 tablespoons psyllium
1 tablespoon gelatine
2 tablespoons poppy seeds
2 teaspoons gluten-free baking powder
5 oz/150g butter
½ cup orange juice

Orange icing
2 cups pure icing sugar
juice of 1 orange
2 tablespoons butter or margarine

1 Preheat the oven to 360°F/180°C. Grease heavily a 12 in/30cm log pan with margarine. Place all the ingredients into a mixing bowl in their listed order and mix well with an electric mixer for about 1 minute and scrape into the prepared pan.

2 Place on the middle shelf in your oven and bake for 35 minutes until just firm to touch. Remove from the oven and while it is still in the tin sprinkle the warm orange juice over the cake. Stand for a few minutes before turning out. When cool ice with orange icing.

3 To make the orange icing, cream the ingredients together and spread on the cooled cake.

This cake will retain moisture for several days if kept in a closed container.

Serves 2–4 • Preparation 15 minutes • Cooking 35 minutes

Pixie custard buns

1 batch of basic bun dough (page 162)
½ cup sultanas
1 red apple, sliced

Custard filling
1 tablespoon margarine
1 tablespoon Lola's superfine flour (page 7)
2 tablespoons sugar
2 tablespoons vanilla essence
4 tablespoons cream cheese
2 tablespoons ground almonds

1 To make the custard filling, melt the margarine in a saucepan, add the flour and cook for 1 minute. Add ½ cup of boiling water and whisk over heat until thick. Whisk in the sugar, vanilla essence, cream cheese and ground almonds. Place in the refrigerator to cool.

2 Preheat oven to 360°F/180°C. You will need two sheets of cling wrap about 12 x 9 in/30 x 22mm. Grease the pixie bun trays. Press the dough out flat between the sheets of cling wrap.

3 Cut out dough circles with a large serrated cutter and press lightly into the pans, making sure that the dough comes up to the top of the pan. Place a few sultanas in the bun and spoon on a tablespoon of custard.

4 Top with a few slices of red apple before sealing with a lid of bun dough. Use a smaller cutter for the lids and drop the lids into a saucer of cold water before placing on top of the filled bun. (This will seal in the custard.) Leave to rise for 30 minutes before baking for 15 minutes.

Custard can be made the previous day.

Serves 4 • Preparation 50 minutes • Cooking 15 minutes

Fairy cakes

4 eggs
7 oz/200g caster sugar
7 oz/200g Lola's all-purpose flour (page 7)
2 oz/60g ground almonds
1 tablespoon vanilla essence
2 tablespoons psyllium
2 tablespoons gelatine
3 teaspoons gluten-free baking powder
7 oz/200g butter or margarine
icing or cream, as desired, for decoration

1 Preheat the oven to 360°F/180°C. Line 24 patty tins with papers. Don't use aluminium tins.
2 Place the ingredients, except the icing, into a mixing bowl in their listed order and mix well with an electric mixer for about 1 minute. Spoon into the prepared patty pans and let rest for 5 minutes to help with the rising of the cakes.
3 Place on the high shelf in your oven and bake for 10 minutes until just firm to touch – don't overcook. Ice or fill with cream as desired.
4 Cakes will retain their moisture for several days kept in a cake tin and will freeze well in foil or a plastic container.

They will dry in the freezer in a plastic bag.

Makes 24 cakes • Preparation 20 minutes • Cooking 10 minutes

Rum balls

2 oz/60g dairy-free margarine
2 tablespoons treacle
2 oz/60g brown sugar
1 tablespoon cocoa
1 tablespoon rum
2 tablespoons almond meal
1 cup mixed chopped raisins and prunes
1 cup chopped mixed nuts: flaked almonds, cashews, walnuts and hazelnuts

1 Place the margarine, treacle and brown sugar in a saucepan and slowly bring to the boil.
2 Remove from the heat and stir in the remaining ingredients. Mix well by hand or in a food processor. Cool and roll into balls. Coat as desired (see below).

No cake or biscuit crumbs are needed to make this recipe. The rum balls can be chocolate-coated or for a dairy-free result, roll in cocoa or coconut.

Serves 2–4 • Preparation 10 minutes • Cooking 10 minutes

Traditional lamingtons

1 teaspoon butter
3½ oz/100g caster sugar
1 teaspoon vanilla essence
3½ oz/100g Lola's all-purpose flour (page 7)
1 teaspoon gluten-free baking powder
3 large eggs

Chocolate icing
7 oz/200g pure icing sugar
1 tablespoon cocoa
1 teaspoon butter
5 oz/150g desiccated coconut
1 teaspoon vanilla essence

1 Preheat the oven to 320 °F/160°C. Prepare a 8 in/20cm square tin by greasing the sides with margarine and placing a layer of baking paper in the bottom of the tin. Place the butter in a small bowl, add the vanilla essence and 3 teaspoons of hot water, and let stand for 1 minute.

3 Place the eggs and caster sugar in a metal bowl and whisk with a wire whisk over a saucepan of hot water until the mixture is warm and slightly frothy. Remove from the heat and continue beating with a rotary or electric beater until the mixture is thick and creamy but not stiff.

4 Carefully sift the flour and baking powder into the egg mixture. Pour the warm butter mix around the sides of the bowl as you continue to fold the mixture. Quickly pour into the prepared cake tin and place in the centre of the oven.

5 Cook for 15 minutes. Let stand in the oven for an extra 5 minutes with the door ajar. Cool the cake and cut into squares. Freeze the squares for about 20 minutes before coating with chocolate icing. Finish by rolling the coated squares in desiccated coconut.

6 To make the chocolate icing, sift the cocoa and icing sugar together into a large bowl. Dissolve the butter in a little hot water, add to the icing sugar and mix to a thin icing. Coat each frozen cake square with the chocolate icing and roll in coconut.

The completed cakes will freeze well.

Serves 4–6 • Preparation 40 minutes • Cooking 20 minutes

Apple and sultana spice bun

1 teaspoon salt
3 tablespoons caster sugar
1 tablespoon gelatine
2 oz/60g mashed potato
1 tablespoon dry yeast
7 oz/200g Lola's bread and pastry flour (page 7)
2½ oz/75g arrowroot
1 tablespoon ground ginger
1 tablespoon mixed spice
1 teaspoon cinnamon
2 eggs
1 chopped apple
5 oz/150g sultanas

1 Grease a ring or saddle tin with some dairy-free margarine. Place 7 oz/200mL cold water into a glass bowl. Add the salt, caster sugar and gelatine; let stand for 1 minute to soften. Heat the gelatine mixture until gelatine dissolves.

2 Whisk the mashed potato in to the warm gelatine mixture. Stir in the yeast and let stand for 3 minutes. Combine the flour, arrowroot and spices. Tip the dry ingredients into the wet mixture and beat in the whisked eggs. Beat the mixture for 1 minute with the electric mixer.

3 Preheat oven to 360°F/180°C. Pour a quarter of the mixture into the bread pan and spread over the base. Sprinkle a quarter of the apple and sultanas over the mixture and top with more batter. Cover the remaining fruit with more dough mixture. Leave to stand for 15 minutes. Place in the centre of the oven and bake for 35 minutes. Remove from the oven and wrap in a tea towel and leave to cool.

Serves 2–4 • Preparation 40 minutes • Cooking 35 minutes

Hot cross buns

2 teaspoons salt
3½ oz/100g caster sugar
1 tablespoon gelatine
2 tablespoons glycerine
2 tablespoons margarine
2 tablespoons instant dry yeast
10 oz/300g Lola's bread and pastry flour
  (page 7)
3½ oz/100g arrowroot
2 oz/60g ground almonds (almond meal)
1 tablespoon mixed spice
1 tablespoon cinnamon

2 teaspoons ground ginger
1 egg
½ cup mixed dried fruit

Cross mix
2 teaspoons psyllium
1 tablespoon sugar
1 tablespoon fine rice four

Bun glaze
1 tablespoon gelatine
2 tablespoons sugar
1 teaspoon mixed spice

1 Preheat the oven to 360°F/180°C. Grease muffin tins or bun trays. Place 1 cup of cold water, salt, sugar and gelatine in a glass bowl. Let stand for 1 minute to soften. Heat in the microwave for 40 seconds.

2 Add the glycerine and margarine to the gelatine mixture. Stir in the yeast. Let stand for 3 minutes. Combine the flour, arrowroot, almond meal and spices in a plastic bag and give a good shake to mix well. Lightly whisk the egg. Tip the dry ingredients into the yeast mixture and add the egg.

3 Beat the mixture for 2 minutes with an electric mixer. Let stand for 10 minutes. Whisk briefly and pour the mixture into a jug. Stand the mixture for another 10 minutes, then whisk again. Quarter fill the bun pans with the mixture. Sprinkle 1 teaspoonful of fruit over the mixture and top with more batter and repeat. Sprinkle the remaining fruit over each bun and top with a small amount of batter. Leave to stand for 15 minutes, until a few bubbles appear. To make the cross mix, sprinkle psyllium on ¼ cup cold water and let stand to thicken. Add sugar and fine rice flour. Pipe crosses on the uncooked buns. Place in the centre of the oven for 30 minutes.

4 To make the bun glaze, boil together the ingredients for 1 minute. Glaze as soon as the buns are cooked

Serves 4–6 • Preparation 40 minutes • Cooking 30 minutes

Date slice

Pastry
1 tablespoon gelatine
1 egg
4 oz/125g butter
2 tablespoons pure icing sugar
10 oz/300g Lola's all-purpose flour
  (page 7)

Filing
7 oz/200g dates
1 tablespoon brown sugar

1 tablespoon water
1 tablespoon golden syrup
1 teaspoon mixed spice

Lemon icing
4 oz/125g sifted pure icing sugar
1 teaspoon melted butter
lemon juice to mix

1 Preheat the oven to 360°F/180°C. Select a shallow 8 in/20cm square ungreased cake tin. Soak the gelatine in ¼ cup cold water, then heat gently until dissolved. Cool. Combine all the remaining pastry ingredients in a food processor and process to form a firm pastry.

2 Divide the pastry and press half the mixture into the tin using your fingers. Roll out the other half of the pastry between two sheets of cling wrap for the top of the slice.

3 Warm the dates slightly over a saucepan of hot water. Combine the remainder of the filling ingredients with the softened dates in a food processor and process into a coarse paste.

4 Spread the filling onto the pastry base in the tin and place the rolled out pastry on the top of the date mixture. Prick the top to allow air to escape and give an even appearance when cooked. Brush with water and sprinkle with sugar. Place in the oven and cook for 20 minutes. Cool in the cake tin.

6 To make the lemon icing, combine all ingredients with 1 tablespoon of boiling water to make a creamy icing and pour onto the slice. Cut into squares to serve.

Serves 2–4 • Preparation 40 minutes • Cooking 20 minutes

Cornish splits

1 teaspoon psyllium
1 teaspoon salt
1 tablespoon dried yeast
1 egg
16 oz/450g Lola's superfine flour (page 7)
1 oz/30g pure icing sugar, sifted
2 tablespoons milk powder
1 tablespoon melted margarine

1 Preheat the oven to 400°F/200°C. Cover a scone tray with baking paper. Place ½ cup of warm water in a large mixing bowl and whisk in the psyllium, salt and yeast. Set aside to rise for 10 minutes while you prepare the other ingredients. In a small bowl whisk the egg. Weigh the flour and set aside 5 oz/150g of it for rolling the splits.

2 Combine the larger portion of flour with the icing sugar and milk powder. Add the beaten egg and melted margarine to the yeast mixture. Set the bowl aside to make egg wash by adding a teaspoon of milk and combining with egg residue.

4 Using a knife to avoid over-mixing add the flour mixture to the liquids and blend using a cutting action for about 1 minute until the flour is incorporated. Cover the bowl and rest for 15 minutes.

5 Add half the remaining flour to the risen dough and work in with the knife. Place the remainder of the flour on a pastry board and tip the dough on it. Lightly knead to incorporate the flour, adding a little more flour if necessary. Press the dough out in a thick slab with your fingers and cut with a small cutter.

6 Place the splits together to support each other on the tray. Brush the tops of the splits with the egg wash and leave to rise for 40 minutes. Bake for 15 minutes until golden and serve with strawberry jam and clotted cream sandwiched in between.

Serves 2 • Preparation 1 hour 10 minutes • Cooking 15 minutes

Almond cookies

3½ oz/100g Lola's all-purpose flour (page 7)
3½ oz/100g sugar
1 teaspoon bicarbonate of soda
1½ oz/45g flaked almonds
1 oz/30g ground almonds
1 oz/30g baby rice cereal
⅓ cup olive oil
1 tablespoon water
3 tablespoons liquid glucose
3 teaspoons vanilla essence
1 teaspoon almond essence

1 Preheat the oven to 320°F/160°C. Cover a baking tray with foil or baking paper. Place the flour, sugar, bicarbonate of soda, flaked almonds, ground almonds and rice cereal into a mixing bowl and combine well.

2 Place the oil, water and glucose into a large saucepan and heat slowly to simmering point. Remove the saucepan from the heat and add the dry ingredients to the oil mixture. Add the vanilla and almond essence, and mix well.

At this stage the cookies can be left in the refrigerator until you wish to cook them. If they are well wrapped they will keep for a week. Remove from refrigerator and leave to reach room temperature before slicing to bake.

3 Turn onto a plastic sheet and roll in a long sausage shape. Slice cross-wise into 16 portions using a sharp knife and place on the baking tray. Cook for about 10–15 minutes until a pale golden colour. Cool on the tray.

Makes 16 cookies • Preparation 25 minutes • Cooking 15 minutes

Gingerbread men

½ teaspoon salt
5 oz/150g Lola's bread and pastry flour (page 7)
2 tablespoon amaranth cereal or brown rice flour
2 oz/60g brown sugar
1 teaspoon baking soda
pinch of tartaric acid
1 tablespoon ground ginger (use less if making for children)
¼ cup olive oil
¼ cup treacle
3 tablespoons fine rice flour

1 Preheat the oven to 300°F/150°C. Line a baking tray with baking paper. Combine the dry ingredients (except the fine rice flour) and mix well. In a saucepan on a gentle heat, bring the oil and treacle to boiling point.
2 Remove from heat and tip in the dry ingredients. Using a wooden spoon, mix well and tip onto a sheet of cling wrap. Knead a few times with the rice flour. Cut into shapes with cookie cutters.
3 Place on the prepared tray. Bake for 15 minutes, then remove from the oven and cool on the tray.

Serves 4 • Preparation 20 minutes • Cooking 15 minutes

Cinnamon squares

3 oz/90g dairy-free margarine
2 teaspoons vanilla essence
5 oz/150g Lola's all purpose flour (page 7)
5 oz/150g sugar
1 tablespoon ground cinnamon, sifted
2 egg yolks
2 tablespoons fine rice flour
2 tablespoons olive oil

1 Preheat the oven to 300°F/150°C. Line a baking tray with baking paper.

2 Place all the ingredients except the rice flour and oil in a mixer and blend for a few minutes until the mixture forms a ball. Tip onto a sheet of cling wrap.

3 Knead a few times with the rice flour, then roll out in a thick slab. Cut into shapes with a square cookie cutter.

4 Place on the prepared tray. Brush with olive oil and bake for 10 minutes. Remove from the oven, sprinkle with cinnamon sugar and cool on the tray.

Serves 2–4 • Preparation 12 minutes • Cooking 10 minutes

Ginger shells

1 tablespoon egg replacer
3 tablespoons olive oil
¼ cup pear concentrate or rice syrup
1 tablespoon vanilla essence
5 oz/150g Lola's all purpose flour (page 7)
1 tablespoon ground ginger
½ teaspoon salt
2 teaspoons gluten-free baking powder
3½ oz/100g xylityol

1 Preheat the oven to 320°F/160°C. Lightly grease a 12-cup shell tray with dairy-free margarine. Place ½ cup warm water in a mixing bowl, add egg replacer and let stand for about 2 minutes.

2 Place the oil in a saucepan with the pear concentrate or rice syrup and warm gently, then add the vanilla and remove from the heat.

3 Combine the flour, ginger, salt and baking powder in a separate bowl. Beat the warm water and egg replacer until creamy, then gradually add the xylitol and beat for a few minutes to form a meringue. Add the oil mix, then fold in the dry ingredients.

4 Spoon the mixture into the prepared tray and bake for 10–15 minutes or until firm to the touch.

Serves 4 • Preparation 15 minutes • Cooking 15 minutes

Tiny teddies

1 tablespoon amaranth cereal
5 oz/150g Lola's all purpose flour (page 7)
1 teaspoon baking soda
1 tablespoon cocoa powder
1 teaspoon ground ginger
¼ cup olive oil
¼ cup rice syrup
2 tablespoons extra-fine rice flour
1 tablespoon vanilla essence

1 Preheat the oven to 300°F/150°C. Line a baking tray with baking paper. Combine all the dry ingredients except the rice flour and mix well. In a saucepan on a gentle heat slowly bring the oil and syrup to boiling point.

2 Remove from heat and tip in the dry ingredients, then the vanilla. Using a wooden spoon mix the cookie mixture well and tip onto a sheet of cling wrap.

3 Knead a few times, using the rice flour if necessary. Roll out in a thick sheet and cut with a tiny teddy cutter.

4 Place on the prepared tray. Bake for 15 minutes, then remove from the oven and cool on the tray.

Serves 4 • Preparation 20 minutes • Cooking 15 minutes

Christmas cookies

¼ cup olive oil
2 tablespoons treacle
10 oz/300g Lola's bread and pastry flour (page 7)
3½ oz/100g caster sugar
2 tablespoons ground ginger
1 tablespoon mixed herbs
1 egg, lightly beaten
white chocolate to decorate

1 Preheat the oven to 300°F/150°C. Cover a tray with baking paper. Place the oil and treacle in a saucepan and gently warm.

2 Remove from the heat and add three-quarters of the flour and the remaining ingredients. Mix well with a wooden spoon.

3 Tip onto a sheet of cling wrap or board and knead the remaining flour into the pastry. Roll out between two sheets of plastic. Cut out in desired shapes and place on the covered tray.

4 Place on the centre shelf in your oven and bake for 10 minutes until just firm to touch. Cool on the tray. White chocolate can be used to dip the tops of cookies.

Serves 2–4 • Preparation 20 minutes • Cooking 10 minutes

Wheat-free Anzacs

2 oz/60g rolled rice flakes
¼ cup olive oil
7 oz/200g sugar
2 tablespoons golden syrup
5 oz/150g Lola's all-purpose flour (page 7)
1 tablespoon mixed spice
3½ oz/100g desiccated coconut
1 teaspoon bicarbonate of soda

1 Preheat the oven to 340°F/170°C. Cover one or two large baking trays with baking paper. Place the rolled rice flakes in a saucepan and pour ½ cup of boiling water over them. Simmer for five minutes.

2 Add the oil, sugar and golden syrup to a medium-sized saucepan and warm gently for a few minutes (for a crisper cookie, bring to the boil). Stir in the warm rice flakes, then add the flour, spice and coconut. Finally, add the bicarbonate of soda dissolved in 1 tablespoon of boiling water and mix this stiff mixture well.

3 Spoon onto the baking paper covered trays allowing room to spread and press down. Bake for 15 minutes and cool on the trays. For a less crisp result, reduce the oven temperature to 300°F/150°C. Store in an airtight container.

Serves 4 • Preparation 25 minutes • Cooking 15 minutes

desserts

No need to hide in a corner when the dessert is dished out. Lola has developed a fantastic series of recipes – all gluten free, to really trap the taste buds. You will enjoy such delights as 'Apple and rhubarb crumble' and 'Pear flan' together with a whole host of tasty delights.

Turkish delight

4 tablespoons gelatine
1½ cups xylitol
¾ cup arrowroot, plus a little to dust
1 tablespoon rosewater essence
½ teaspoon beetroot powder
icing sugar to dust

1 Grease an 7 x 10 x 1 in/18 x 24 x 3cm deep slab tin with margarine, then line with baking paper.
2 Place 3 cups water in a saucepan and sprinkle the gelatine on top. Add the xylitol to the water and gelatine and place on a medium heat, whisking with a wire whisk until the mixture comes to a boil and the gelatine and xylitol have dissolved. Continue simmering for about 2 minutes.
3 Remove from the heat. Mix the arrowroot with ½ cup cold water and while stirring the hot syrup, pour the arrowroot into the mixture to thicken it. Flavour with the rosewater essence.
4 Dissolve the beetroot powder in a little warm water and add to the mixture. Pour into the lined tray. Refrigerate overnight, then cut into cubes and dust with a mix of icing sugar and arrowroot.

Serves 2–4 • Preparation 10 minutes • Cooking 8 minutes

Fresh fruit flans

Pastry
½ cup olive oil
2 tablespoons liquid glucose or rice syrup
3½ oz/100g Lola's bread and pastry flour
  (page 7)
1 tablespoon baby rice cereal

Créme patisserie
2 oz/60g butter
3 tablespoons Lola's bread and pastry
  flour (page 7)
1 teaspoon almond essence
2 teaspoons vanilla essence
2 oz/60g caster sugar

1 egg
1 cup milk
½ cup full cream

Topping
1 small can apricot halves
½ cup apricot syrup
5 oz/150g strawberries
3 kiwi fruit, sliced

Fruit glaze
1 tablespoon gelatine
½ cup fruit syrup

1 To make the pastry, preheat the oven to 320°F/160°C. Warm the olive oil and glucose and stir in the flour and rice cereal. Tip onto a sheet of cling wrap and knead lightly. Leave to cool. Roll out between two sheets of plastic to fit six patty pans or one 8 in/20cm plate. Bake the pastry for 15–20 minutes.

2 To make the créme patisserie, cream the butter, flour, essences, sugar and egg together. Heat the milk on a low heat to near boiling, but do not boil. Tip the hot milk into the creamy mixture and whisk well to combine the ingredients. Return the mixture to the heat and cook for a few minutes until thickened. Remove the custard from the saucepan and set aside to cool. Whip the cream and fold into the cooled custard.

3 To make the fruit glaze, sprinkle gelatine on fruit syrup and leave to stand until the gelatine is soft. Place the mixture in a bowl over boiling water until the gelatine syrup is clear.

4 Fill the cooled pastry shells with créme patisserie, piling it high to support the fruit. Arrange the fruit over the créme patisserie and glaze it with a pastry brush and warm glaze.

Serves 4 • Preparation 30 minutes • Cooking 15 minutes

Pear fritters with low-sugar caramel sauce

1 tablespoon egg replacer
1 teaspoon gelatine or agar powder
2 tablespoons xylitol
1 teaspoon vanilla essence
3½ oz/100g superfine flour (page 7)
1 teaspoon gluten-free baking powder
2 cups olive oil
1 large pear, cored and cut crosswise into
  thick slices
cinnamon

Low-sugar caramel sauce
2 sauce blocks (page 9)
5 oz/150g dairy-free margarine
½ cup rice syrup
2 teaspoons caramel essence

1 To make the sauce, place 1 cup boiling water in a saucepan and add the sauce blocks. When the blocks have melted, stir over a low heat until you have a thickened sauce, then set aside to cool.

2 Melt the margarine in a saucepan over low heat, stir in the rice syrup and cook for about 2 minutes until the mixture turns a golden caramel colour. Add the sauce to the margarine mixture and stir in the caramel essence. Beat well until smooth and creamy. Keep warm while you make the fritters.

3 To make the fritters, beat the egg replacer, gelatine or agar and ⅔ cup warm water with an electric beater until thick and frothy. Add the xylitol a little at a time and continue beating for a further minute. Stir in the vanilla, flour and baking powder. Whisk well until the mixture is a smooth batter.

4 Heat the oil in a deep pan. Thinly coat the fruit with batter – if the batter is too thick, add a little more warm water. Gently lower the coated fruit into the hot oil. Turn once while cooking and cook until golden. Remove from the oil and drain on absorbent paper. Sprinkle with cinnamon and extra xylitol and serve warm with the caramel sauce.

Serves 4 • Preparation 30 minutes • Cooking 10 minutes

Baked rice pudding

2 tablespoons dairy-free margarine
2 tablespoons superfine flour (page 7)
1 cup rice milk
2 tablespoons sugar
1 teaspoon vanilla essence
½ cup boiled rice
1 tablespoon brown sugar
cinnamon

1 Melt the margarine and stir in the flour – cook for a few minutes until the mixture slides in the saucepan.
2 Add the rice milk and whisk well over the heat to produce a thick custard. Add the sugar, vanilla and cooked rice.
3 Spoon the mixture into ovenproof serving dishes and sprinkle with brown sugar and a little cinnamon. Grill for 5 minutes to brown the topping.

Traditional baked rice does not cook well with rice milk but this method gives a creamy pudding.

Serves 2 • Preparation 10 minutes • Cooking 8 minutes

Lemon meringue pie

4 oz/125g Lola's bread and pastry flour (page 7)
2 oz/60g dairy-free margarine
1 egg yolk
1 tablespoon rice syrup

Lemon filling
2 oz/60g sugar
juice of 2 lemons
zest of 1 lemon, grated
2 tablespoons tapioca starch
2 egg yolks

Meringue
3 egg whites
3½ oz/100g caster sugar

1 Preheat the oven to 360°F/160°C. Place the flour, margarine, egg yolk, rice syrup and enough cold water to mix in a food processor. Process until it forms a ball. Tip out and knead lightly, then press the pastry into an ungreased 8 in/20cm tart ring with a removable base. Bake the pastry for about 20 minutes. Set aside until cool.

2 Place 1 cup water, the sugar, lemon juice and zest in a saucepan, heat until near boiling point, then remove from heat. Mix the tapioca starch with a little cold water and stir into the juice mixture.

3 Return to the heat and stir until the mixture thickens. Whisk the yolks and add them to the mixture, stir well for about 1 minute over the heat.

4 Pour the lemon filling into the cooked pastry case. Beat the egg whites until they are stiff, then gradually add the caster sugar, beating until it has completely dissolved. Spoon on top of the lemon filling and place in the oven for about 15 minutes.

Serves 4 • Preparation 25 minutes • Cooking 35 minutes

Apple and rhubarb crumble

3 large cooking apples, thinly sliced
½ cup sugar or substitute
small bunch rhubarb, sliced crosswise

Topping
2 oz/60g butter
3½ oz/100g Lola's all-purpose flour (page 7)
3½ oz/100g sugar
3½ oz/100g almond meal

1 Preheat the oven to 400°F/200°C. Place the apples in a greased pie dish. Sprinkle with sugar or substitute.

2 Cook the rhubarb gently with sugar to taste in a saucepan.

3 To make the topping, combine the topping ingredients together.

4 Tip the cooked juicy rhubarb over the raw apple and sprinkle with the topping. Bake for 20 minutes.

This dessert can be made with canned or fresh apple, but the rhubarb needs to be cooked separately for the best result.

Serves 4 • Preparation 20 minutes • Cooking 20 minutes

Pear and passionfruit meringue

3 large ripe pears
3 passionfruit
3 egg whites
1 cup caster sugar
1 teaspoon vanilla essence
1 teaspoon cream of tartar
cinnamon sugar

1 Preheat the oven to 360°F/180°C. Peel and quarter the pears and place the pieces in an ovenproof dish. Squeeze the pulp of the passionfruit over the pears.
2 Beat the egg whites until stiff, then gradually add the caster sugar a little at a time, beating well in between each addition. Beat in the vanilla and finally add the cream of tartar.
3 Pile the mixture over fruit and spread, making sure that you seal the edges of the meringue to the dish – this prevents the meringue sweating.
4 Turn the oven temperature down to 300°F/150°C. Sprinkle the meringue with cinnamon sugar and place in the oven. Bake until firm, about 30 minutes. Serve with dairy-free custard (page 228).

Serves 2–4 • Preparation 25 minutes • Cooking 30 minutes

Apple sponge dessert

4 large cooking apples, peeled and sliced
3½ oz/100g sugar
1 tablespoon butter
1 large egg
3½ oz/100g Lola's bread and pastry flour (page 7)
2 oz/60g caster sugar
1 teaspoon gluten-free baking powder

1 Preheat the oven to 360°F/180°C. Cook the apples with the sugar and ¼ cup of cold water until soft. Place the cooked apples into a greased ovenproof dish about 8 in/20cm in diameter.
2 Place the butter in ¼ cup of hot water to melt. Beat the egg and caster sugar together until thick and creamy. Blend the flour and baking powder into the creamy egg mixture. Add the cooled water and butter mixture to the bowl and stir to form a light batter.
4 Pour the batter onto the hot apple and bake in the oven for 10–15 minutes or until the batter is firm. Serve warm with cream or ice cream.

The batter mixture should be thin enough to pour easily onto the apples. As these flours often vary in consistency, it may be necessary to add a little more warm water to the mixture. Instead of apples, try fresh mulberries sprinkled with sugar.

Serves 4 • Preparation 25 minutes • Cooking 15 minutes

Caramelised pear flan

2 tablespoons margarine
¼ cup brown sugar
1 large pear, peeled, quartered and sliced into wedges
2 eggs
⅓ cup caster sugar
2½ oz/75g Lola's bread and pastry flour (page 7)
2 teaspoons gluten-free baking powder

Dairy-free custard
¼ cup sugar
2 Lola's sauce blocks (page 9)
1 egg, beaten
2 teaspoons vanilla essence

1 Preheat the oven to 360°F/180°C. Liberally grease a 8 in/20cm cake tin, using all the margarine. Sprinkle the brown sugar over the margarine. Overlap the pear slices in the tin in a circular pattern.

2 Whisk the eggs and sugar until creamy, add the flour and baking powder, and pour over the pears. Place the flan in the oven and bake for 25 minutes. Turn out immediately and serve warm with dairy-free custard.

3 To make the dairy-free custard, bring 1 cup of water and sugar to the boil, add the sauce blocks and let stand until blocks soften. Return to the heat and whisk until the mixture thickens. Add the beaten egg and vanilla. Stir gently over the heat for 1 minute to cook the egg. Do not let the custard boil.

Serves 4 • Preparation 25 minutes • Cooking 30 minutes

Yellow peach strudel

4 large yellow peaches, peeled and sliced
¾ cup sugar
1 tablespoon gelatine
3½ oz/100g butter
1 egg
10 oz/300g Lola's all-purpose flour (page 7)
2 tablespoons pure icing sugar

1 Preheat the oven to 360°F/180°C. Soak the gelatine in ¼ cup cold water, then heat gently until dissolved. Cool. Combine all the pastry ingredients with the gelatine mixture in a food processor and process to form a firm pastry.

2 Divide the pastry and press half the mixture into a shallow 8 in/20cm square ungreased cake pan with your fingers. Place the peeled and sliced peaches on the pastry base, then sprinkle with ½ cup sugar.

3 Roll out the other half of the pastry for the top of the strudel. Cut pastry into strips and use to form a lattice over the fresh peach slices.

4 Glaze with the reserved egg white and sprinkle with remaining sugar. Place in the oven and bake for 35 minutes. Serve with cream.

Peaches can be peeled easily if they are blanched in boiling water for a few minutes and then placed in cold water. Reserve a tiny amount of egg white to glaze the top of the lattice.

Serves 4 • Preparation 40 minutes • Cooking 35 minutes

Baked cheesecake

Base
2 oz/60g butter
1 tablespoon honey
4 oz/125g crushed wheat-free biscuit crumbs or gluten-free corn cereal
1½ oz/45g desiccated coconut

Filling
16 oz/500g firm cream cheese
8 oz/250g soft cream or ricotta cheese
1 tablespoon sour cream
7 oz/200g caster sugar
2 eggs
2 tablespoons vanilla essence
sprinkle of nutmeg

Topping
1 cup cream
whipped and grated chocolate or fresh fruit

1 Preheat oven to 300°F/150°C.
2 To make the base, melt the butter and honey over a low heat and mix with the cereal or crumbs. You may need a little hot water if the cereal is dry. Combine with the coconut and press into a removable base cake tin.
3 To make the filling, beat the cheeses and sour cream with the caster sugar until creamy. Add the eggs one at a time and whip on high speed. Add the vanilla essence to the mixture and pour into the uncooked crumb case. Sprinkle with nutmeg and place into the centre of the oven for 1 hour. Turn the heat off and leave in the oven for an additional hour to set.
4 Serve cold, with whipped cream, fresh fruit or grated chocolate.

Don't worry if the cheesecake has a crack in the top, cream will cover it.

Serves 4 • Preparation 35 minutes • Cooking 1 hour

Continental sponge

2 eggs
2½ oz/75g caster sugar
2½ oz/75g Lola's all-purpose flour (page 7)
2 teaspoon gluten-free baking powder
2 teaspoons margarine

1   Preheat the oven to 360°F/180°C. Grease a 8 in/20cm flan tin and dust with flour or line with baking paper.
2   Whisk the eggs and caster sugar over hot water until they are just warm and bubbly. Using an electric beater, beat until the mixture is thick and creamy but not stiff. Fold the flour and baking powder into the egg mixture.
3   Melt the margarine in 2 tablespoons of boiling water and pour down the inside of the bowl containing the batter. Turn the mixture with a wire whisk, being careful not to over-mix as this will release the air and flatten the sponge.
4   Pour into the tin and gently move the mixture with a spatula so that a small depression is made in the centre of the cake. Place in the centre of the oven and bake for 15 minutes. Stand for 5 minutes before turning out.

This recipe is used for the berry gateau on page 236. It freezes well if foil-wrapped and so is a great standby. Cut in squares and serve filled with warm stewed apple to make a quick dessert.

Serves 2–4 • Preparation 30 minutes • Cooking 20 minutes

Berry Gâteau

1 continental sponge (page 235)
8 oz/250g strawberries
3½ oz/100g blueberries or 1 can mixed berries
3½ oz/100g sugar
3½ oz/100g raspberry jam
2 egg whites
7 oz/200g icing sugar

1 When the sponge is cold, using a serrated knife, slice it carefully into three, commencing at the top.

2 Select about eight of the best strawberries from the punnet and set side. Slice the remaining strawberries, add the blueberries and sauté with the sugar. Spread the berry sauté mixture onto two layers. If using canned berries, you will need to strain them and thicken the juice with a tablespoon of cornflour, then stir in the strained berries.

3 Preheat the oven to 400°F/200°C. Stack up and coat the top of the sponge with warmed berry jam.

4 Place the egg whites and icing sugar into a bowl and heat over hot water until the mixture is warm and shiny. Beat with an electric mixer until the mixture is stiff enough to pipe. Decorate or spread the meringue to cover the cake.

5 Bake the meringue-covered gateau in the oven for about 15 minutes. Finish with the selected strawberries dipped in berry jam. Serve with berry coulis and yoghurt for a low cholesterol dessert.

Serves 4–6 • Preparation 35 minutes • Cooking 15 minutes

Christmas pudding

1 teaspoon nutmeg
4 oz/125g currants
5 oz/150g sultanas
5 oz/150g raisins
1 oz/30g walnuts, chopped
1 oz/30g slivered almonds

¼ cup rum
4 oz/125g butter
4 oz/125g brown sugar
1 tablespoon golden syrup
5 oz/150g Lola's all-purpose
   flour (page 7)

2 oz/60g almond meal
1 teaspoon mixed spice
1 teaspoon bicarbonate of
   soda
2 eggs

1 Combine the fruit and nuts in a large bowl and sprinkle with the rum. Cover and stand overnight. Half fill a large saucepan with water, place a saucer or rack in the bottom, lid the saucepan and bring to a boil.

2 Mix together the butter, brown sugar and golden syrup. Add the flour, almond meal, spices and bicarbonate of soda to the fruit mixture. Lightly beat the eggs and combine all the ingredients, gently. The mixture should hold its shape – if not, add a little more flour.

3 Grease a pudding basin with margarine and spoon the mixture into the basin. Cover with a loose piece of foil and cook for 2 hours on the first day in the saucepan with the lid on. Heat up on the day of serving.

4 Reheat the pudding in a large saucepan of boiling water. To flame the pudding in a traditional way it is necessary to first warm a spirit. Either brandy or whisky will flame well. Be careful if you are warming over an open flame as it will catch alight easily. Once alight pour the pudding over the pudding very carefully.

Serves 6–8 • Preparation 1 hour 15 minutes • Cooking 2 hour

Lemon delicious pudding

2 tablespoons margarine
7 oz/200g sugar
zest and juice of 2 lemons
4 eggs, separated
3 tablespoons Lola's bread and pastry flour (page 7)
1 cup milk

1 Preheat the oven to 360°F/180°C. Grease a small casserole dish with margarine. Cream together the margarine, sugar, zest and egg yolks.

2 Add the sifted flours, milk and juice – stir to combine. Separately beat the egg whites until stiff and fold into the mixture.

3 Pour into the prepared casserole dish and place in the centre of the oven.

4 Cook for approximately 20–25 minutes until the sponge is firm to touch. As there is custard underneath the sponge, the pudding will be a little wobbly when it is cooked. Serve warm with cream or ice cream.

This dessert can be made in individual dishes for easy serving.

Serves 4 • Preparation 20 minutes • Cooking 25 minutes

Plum jam pudding

margarine to grease the basin
2 tablespoons plum jam
2 oz/60g butter
2 oz/60g sugar
1 egg
2½ oz/75g Lola's all-purpose flour (page 7)
1 teaspoon gluten-free baking powder
1 tablespoon milk

1 Place a saucepan that will fit a 5 x 2 in/13 x 6cm deep fluted pudding basin, on to boil with enough water to come halfway up the pudding basin. Make sure that you have a tight fitting lid for the saucepan.

2 Grease the pudding basin well with margarine, and cut a piece of greaseproof paper large enough to fit the top of the basin. The paper should be larger than the basin so that it will not let any water in when the pudding is steaming.

3 Place the plum jam in the bottom of the greased pudding basin. Cream the butter, sugar and egg together until fluffy. Fold in the sifted flour and baking powder. Stir in the milk and pour into the pudding basin. Lower the pudding into the boiling water. Loosely lay the greaseproof paper on top of the pudding.

4 Place the lid on the saucepan and keep the water boiling for about 40 minutes. When cooked, turn the pudding out onto a plate and serve with custard or ice cream.

Serves 3 • Preparation 25 minutes • Cooking 40 minutes

sauces, stuffing & pickles

To complete the meal one will require a knowledge of great sauces and gravies. In this chapter Lola has developed several classic sauces all gluten free and designed to give great taste to your dish.

Basic stock

2–4 lb/1–2kg beef soup bones
vegetable peelings

1 Preheat oven to 400°F/200°C.
2 Place the beef bones (depending on
   the size of your boiler), on an oven tray
   and bake for about 2 hours.
3 Remove the browned bones from the
   oven and place in a large boiler.
4 Cover with water and boil for about
   3 hours with saved vegetable peelings.
5 Stand overnight to let the flavour
   develop and then remove any fat, the
   bones and vegetable peelings.
6 The stock is now ready for use and
   can be frozen in cup-sized blocks until
   required (tea cups are suitable
   for freezing). Just remove the blocks
   when frozen and place in a plastic bag
   or container.

**When you are planning to make stock,
wash your vegetables well and save
any peelings in the days before, then
refrigerate them until you are ready to
make the stock.**

Makes about 5 cups • Preparation 10
minutes • Cooking 5 hours

Basic sauce

Two sauce blocks (page 9) will thicken
1 cup of liquid for a thin sauce or soup
base. Use three blocks for a thick sauce.
Bring the liquid to the boil, add the frozen
blocks and set aside until the blocks melt.
When the blocks have melted, whisk the
mixture and return to the heat. Stir until
thickened.

**Use this sauce for pasta or vegetable
dishes, or as a base for the following
soups.**

Cheese sauce – Add grated cheese.

Cream sauce – Add milk powder, or sour
cream, or yoghurt.

Cream soups – Soups can be made with a
water base and gluten-free stock cubes.

Mushroom cream soup – Add sautéed
mushrooms to the basic sauce.

Green asparagus soup – Blend 1 can
of green asparagus and juice with the
basic sauce.

Cauliflower soup – Blend cooked
cauliflower with the basic sauce. Use
sauce blocks to suspend the vegetables in
potato and leek, or pumpkin soup.

Tangy tomato sauce

28 oz/800g canned diced Roma tomatoes
3½ oz/100g sugar
2 teaspoons salt
pinch of citric acid
1 teaspoon turmeric
1 sprig thyme, leaves picked
grated zest of 1 lime
juice of 2 limes

1 Place all the ingredients except the lime zest and juice in a saucepan and boil rapidly for 10 minutes to reduce the liquid.
2 Blend the mixture to a smooth sauce and add the lime zest and juice.

If you want a thicker sauce with a less spicy flavour, add 1 cup of water and thicken with a sauce block (page 9).

Makes about 2 cups • Preparation 15 minutes • Cooking 15 minutes

Green pepper sauce

1 cup stock
2 sauce blocks (page 9)
1 teaspoon green peppercorns
1 tablespoon sour cream

1 Heat the stock, then remove from the heat and add the sauce blocks. When they have softened, return to the heat and whisk into a smooth sauce.
2 Place the sauce, green peppercorns and sour cream into a blender and blend until smooth.
3 Leave to stand for at least 30 minutes for flavour to develop. Reheat to serve.

If you have a china sauce boat, place the sauce in the boat and re-heat in the microwave at serving time.

Makes about 1 cup • Preparation 10 minutes • Cooking 45 minutes

Beef pasta sauce

8 oz/250g gluten-free minced beef
4 oz/125g minced pork
1 sauce block (page 9)
14 oz/400g canned diced tomatoes
1 sprig thyme, leaves picked
1 tablespoon basil leaves, chopped
2 teaspoons salt
2 teaspoons freshly ground black pepper

1 Place the meat in an ungreased hot pan and spread to cover the base of the pan.

2 Cook over a high heat until it starts to smell like barbecued meat – do not stir it or you will lose the juices.

3 When the meat is nutty brown, sprinkle the pan with water and turn with a spatula.

4 Continue cooking in this method over high heat until the meat is a rich brown colour.

5 Add 1 cup water, bring to the boil, add the sauce block and stir until the sauce is thick.

6 Add the tomatoes, herbs and seasoning. Adjust with a little more hot water if too thick.

Makes about 2 cups • Preparation 20 minutes • Cooking 15 minutes

Mushroom pasta sauce

8 oz/250g fresh mushrooms
1 teaspoon butter
1 cup chicken or vegetable stock
1 teaspoon dried onion
2 sauce blocks (page 9)
salt and freshly ground black pepper

1 Chop or slice the mushrooms and sauté for a few minutes in a frying pan with a teaspoon of butter. Set aside.

2 Place the stock in a saucepan, add the onion and bring to the boil.

3 Remove from the heat and place the sauce blocks in the boiling stock to melt.

4 Whisk the mixture and return to the heat, stirring until thickened (about 1 minute).

5 Add the sautéed mushrooms to the sauce and season with the pepper and salt.

Makes about 2 cups • Preparation 20 minutes • Cooking 15 minutes

Asian dipping sauce

3 tablespoons plum jam
juice of 1 lemon
juice of 1 lime
1cm piece fresh ginger, grated
1 teaspoon ground ginger
2 tablespoons brown sugar

1 Blend together with a stick blender.
   Optional – garnish with lemon zest.
   Keep refrigerated in a jar.

Makes about ½ cup • Preparation 5
minutes • Cooking none

Hollandaise

½ cup white wine or cider vinegar
1 slice of onion
2 bay leaves
1 teaspoon black peppercorns
4 oz/125g butter
4 egg yolks
juice of 1 lemon

1 Place the vinegar, onion, bay leaves
   and peppercorns in a saucepan and boil
   until the mixture reduces by about a
   third. Strain and set aside to cool.

2 Soften the butter, but do not melt
   it. This can be done successfully in
   a microwave on low temperature or
   simply leave it out of the refrigerator in
   warm weather.

3 Place the egg yolks into a metal basin
   and whisk in the vinegar mixture.
   Whisk this mixture over a saucepan of
   hot water until it just begins to thicken.

4 Remove from the heat and whisk in
   about 1 tablespoon of the softened
   butter, using a wire whisk or an electric
   beater.

5 Continue beating, adding butter a little
   at a time until the mixture is thick and
   creamy. Beat in the lemon juice to taste.

Makes about 1 cup • Preparation 20
minutes • Cooking 10 minutes

Mayonnaise

4 egg yolks
1 tablespoon caster sugar
1 teaspoon salt
1 teaspoon powdered mustard
½ cup olive oil
1 tablespoon white wine vinegar

1 Using an electric blender, process the egg yolks, sugar, salt and mustard for about 1 minute.
2 With the machine running, slowly pour in the oil, then add the vinegar and beat until thick.

Keep this mayonnaise in the refrigerator. To make a lighter salad cream for coleslaw dressing, add 1 tablespoon water to the finished mayonnaise.

Makes about 1 cup • Preparation 10 minutes • Cooking none

Lemon butter

4 eggs
7 oz/200g sugar
4 oz/125g butter at room temperature
juice and zest of 2 lemons

1 Whisk the eggs and sugar together in a bowl and beat in the lemon juice.
2 Place the bowl over a saucepan of simmering water and whisk until the mixture has thickened.
3 Remove from the heat and beat in the softened butter, a little at a time.
4 Return to the heat and whisk for 1 minute. Bottle and seal in screwtop jars while hot. Keep refrigerated and serve with pikelets or in tarts.

This is a delicious filling for tarts or spread for pikelets.

Makes about 1 cup • Preparation 10 minutes • Cooking 10 minutes

Chocolate sauce

2 tablespoons cocoa
4 oz/125g brown sugar
4 oz/125g butter
1 tablespoon golden syrup
1 can condensed milk
1 teaspoon vanilla essence

1 Sift the cocoa into a bowl with the brown sugar; melt the butter and gradually stir into the sugar and cocoa. Add the golden syrup and place the mixture in a saucepan over a low heat.

2 Stir constantly until the mixture forms a rich fudge mixture.

3 Beat in the condensed milk with a wooden spoon and continue cooking for a few minutes until the sauce is smooth, being careful not to burn the mixture, then add vanilla essence. Thin the mixture with a little warm water or brandy.

This is an ideal sauce for chocolate ice cream cake using the continental sponge recipe on page 235.

Makes about 1 cup • Preparation 10 minutes • Cooking 10 minutes

Creamy caramel sauce

½ cup butter
½ cup brown sugar
1 can condensed milk
1 tablespoon golden syrup
3 tablespoons brandy

1 Melt the butter in a saucepan over low heat, stir in the brown sugar and cook for about 1 minute, until the mixture turns a light golden caramel colour.

2 Stir in the condensed milk and the golden syrup and cook for about 30 seconds over a very low heat.

3 Remove from the heat and stir in the brandy and enough water to thin to the consistency that you require.

Serve warm in tiny individual ceramic pots with a platter of fresh fruit pieces, or poured over waffles, banana fritters or ice cream.

Makes about 1 cup • Preparation 10 minutes • Cooking 10 minutes

Sweet mustard pickles

7 oz/200g cauliflower flowerets
2 medium-sized chokos, finely chopped
3 large onions, sliced
4 or 5 green tomatoes, coarsely chopped
1 cup brown cider vinegar
1½ cups white wine vinegar
¾ cup brown sugar
2 tablespoons turmeric

1 tablespoon dried mustard
2 tablespoons cornflour
2 tablespoons potato flour
1 teaspoon powdered ginger

Brine
½ cup salt
2 cups hot water

1 Add the salt to the hot water and stir until dissolved. Let cool slightly and pour over the vegetable and leave to stand overnight. If you like pickles chunky, then you can leave larger pieces. The total weight of the vegetables should be approximately 2 lb/1kg. Next day, wash the brine from the vegetables under cold water.

2 Place the vinegars and sugar into a large saucepan and add the vegetables. Bring to the boil and cook for approximately 20 minutes, until the vegetables are tender but still firm.

3 Mix together ½ cup cold water with the turmeric, mustard, cornflour, potato flour and ginger to form a paste. Thicken the vegetables by stirring the paste into the vegetables. Cook for a few minutes until the mixture thickens and then pour into sterilised jars and seal immediately with screwtop lids. Turn upside down to cool. Check the seal – the top should be concave when the pickle is cold, if not, remove the lid and heat again by placing the jar of pickles in a saucepan of water. Bring to the boil and seal again as before.

Makes about **6 cups** • Preparation 30 minutes + Standing time • Cooking 40 minutes

Vegetable stuffing

1 cup cauliflower flowerets
1 cup green beans, sliced
½ cup mozzarella cheese, grated
salt and freshly ground black pepper
½ cup onion, chopped
½ cup water chestnut, sliced

1 Place the cauliflower and beans in a saucepan, cover with cold water and bring to the boil.

2 Drain the vegetables and add the cheese, salt and pepper, onion and the water chestnuts. Use as desired to stuff veal or chicken.

Makes about 3 cups • Preparation 10 minutes • Cooking 10 minutes

Pistachio stuffing

4 oz/125g cooked rice
2½ oz/75g chopped bacon
1 small onion
1 teaspoon mixed herbs
2 oz/60g shelled pistachio nuts
salt and freshly ground black pepper

1 Combine all the ingredients and mix well.

This delicious stuffing can be used in poultry, pork or veal. Wheat-free breadcrumbs may be used to replace some of the cooked rice.

Makes about 1 cup • Preparation 10 minutes • Cooking 10 minutes

Index